Reading Alive!

Gwen Gawith

A&C Black · London

A CIP catalogue record for this book is available
from the British Library

ISBN 0–7136–3203–8

A&C Black (Publishers) Limited
35 Bedford Row, London WC1R 4JH

This edition © 1990 A&C Black (Publishers) Limited

First published 1989 Longman Paul Limited, New Zealand,
with the title Reading Alive! © 1989 Longman Paul Limited

Acknowledgement
The cover illustration is by Doffy Weir

Contents

WHO?

Reading Alive! is intended for **teachers** to use with students of all abilities in the 8–14 age range.

WHAT?

Reading Alive! is intended to support teachers' attempts to encourage an interest in reading in all children. It is NOT a reading programme, and it does NOT imply that every time a book is read an activity must be completed. There are many books and many times when it is best to let the book speak for itself, to do nothing and to require nothing to be done! With other books and on other occasions it may be useful to let students choose from activities which provide a focus for individual or group work, sharing and discussion. The activities are not 'springboard time-fillers' i.e. leading from the book out to something enjoyable but unrelated. They are all carefully designed to lead back into the book, to encourage re-reading, thinking, discussion and analysis. They are intended to show students how to take responsibility for themselves as readers; to choose from a range and repertoire of reading styles and approaches; to relate reading input to reading output.

WHY?

Behind *Reading Alive!* is the assumption that reading is much more than finding out what happened next; that the emotional satisfactions of book story are different from screen story. However, children without a background rich in print story need help to explore these satisfactions, and to understand that to get reward from reading, the reader has to invest effort, energy, and emotion in reading. This is not to say that there is no place for instant gratification 'candyfloss' reading. We all need it. We all do it. The point is to be able to **choose** what to invest for what reward. The activities are designed to pattern how that investment works for the reader.

HOW?

How you use *Reading Alive!* will depend on the age and reading experience of the children you teach. Using it like a reading programme and insisting that students complete activities will have the opposite effect from that intended. Providing a context for lots of reading and sharing and discussion of books, and giving students the opportunity to use these response triggers when they want to, will help your students to grow as readers.

Foreword

Two years ago I wrote an enthusiastic introduction to Gwen Gawith's *Library Alive!* which promoted reading and research in the school library. I am equally delighted now to welcome its companion, *Reading Alive!* It couldn't have come at a better time.

The introduction of the National Curriculum for English is making us all look closely at what to do in the name of 'Reading'. Attainment Target 2 for Reading tells us, quite simply, that we should be concerned with: 'The development of the ability to read, understand and respond to all types of writing, as well as the development of information retrieval strategies for the purposes of study'.

How in practical classroom terms to encourage and nurture that development remains the question to be answered. Are we doing it already? What, if anything, should we change? Could we do it better?

Some things about reading are clearly asserted in the proposals and statements of the English Working Group ('the Cox committee'), the National Curriculum Council and the two Secretaries of State who have been involved.

> Reading is a quest for meaning which requires the reader to be an active participant.

> Readers learn about reading by doing it, by being engrossed in books, by getting pleasure and satisfaction from it.

> Independent reading is crucial to reading development.

> There are many kinds of writing to be read but an 'active involvement with literature' is essential.

> Literature has personal and social value as well as contributing to language and literacy development.

So can we just let children loose in the Literature section of the library and give them time to read? Experience suggests that it's more complicated than that. Most teachers of 8–14 year olds will tell of pupils who don't know how to be 'engrossed', who have never seen books as a source of satisfaction and pleasure (rather the opposite). They tell also of pupils who restrict their reading to 'pulp fiction', who give the thumbs down to books with lots of description, slow beginnings, complex narratives or ambiguous endings. There are even reports of the elite band, the 'literary readers' getting stuck on a plateau, not knowing where to go next.

To ensure development in reading we have to intervene positively in the process. And it's a complex and subtle process – as easy for our interventions to be negative as positive. Read 'Thirty Ways to Kill Reading' (page 6) to see how, unthinkingly, we often confound our own best efforts. The climate we create has to be right for readers. So has the reading material we provide. Programmes of study and attainment targets cannot be covered by relying on expensively packaged reading schemes complete with 'comprehension' activities, or on English Course Books of selected literary extracts for 'language work'. Professor Cox's English Working Group urges us to select fiction in which the story is 'capable of interpretation at a number of different levels so that children can return to the book time and time again with renewed enjoyment at finding something new.'

There we are again. Even if we can provide the books how do we ensure that readers will 'find something new', will possess the key that opens the way to those 'different levels of interpretation'?

We learn to read by reading. To learn to read more demanding texts we need the opportunity to share and compare with others the meanings we have found, to validate our own responses, to have the support of more experienced readers. Time to read is important but so is time to engage in the kind of talk that helps to clarify and refine what we think. It is this process of reflecting on what we read and how we read it that teaches us more about reading and ourselves as readers. I say 'we' because this is not confined to children or classrooms. 'Real' readers never stop learning.

In classrooms, with relatively inexperienced readers, some structure is useful. Activities which enable readers to make visible the processes of their reading and responses are invaluable because they allow these processes to be recognised and considered. Many of the activities in *Reading Alive!* provide just such support – one reason why this book is so welcome. In recent years, reading logs and response journals have been increasingly used in junior and secondary English classes, providing a unique insight into the development of the reading process for teacher and reader alike. Thoughtfully devised activities of this kind, which support readers and assist teachers in formative assessment, will need to become a regular feature of all classrooms.

Reading Alive! includes activities ideal for recording responses and leading on to the keeping of more extended logs or journals. In addition, there are activities which can be used across the age range to:
    develop awareness of authors
    explore language and how it delights us and influences us
    develop empathy
    focus attention on characterisation, genre, style, how stories are patterned and constructed, the writer/reader relationship.

All offer a basis for talk, collaboration and group work. All are clearly relevant to the National Curriculum for English, as you can see from the chapter and verse extracts on page 5. They were not, though, devised specifically with the National Curriculum in mind. Gwen Gawith was a librarian for many years and is now a College Lecturer in New Zealand. The activities were trialled in classrooms before *Reading Alive!* was first published. Students responded with enthusiasm. Gwen extends her thanks to the teachers who took part in 'Response to Fiction' workshops, in particular for the activities (like 'Castaway Character' and 'Goodies and Baddies') which developed out of the workshops. What lies behind *Reading Alive!* is Gwen Gawith's passionate belief in the importance of reading and the value of literature for young people. 'The ability to read competently, confidently, flexibly and fluently is power' she writes. 'To choose not to exercise that option is your right. If you cannot do it, you do not have the option of choosing, and your power in society is reduced.' She rejects 'the functional/recreational model' which limits our view of reading and suggests that to promote reading always as fun can be counterproductive.

As we concentrate our energies on Attainment Targets and worry about SATs, Gwen's concern for readers reminds us not to lose sight of what it's all for. What does it mean to be a 'real' reader? A 'real' reader feels at home with all kinds of texts, understands that there are many different ways of reading, as many different reading styles and strategies as there are purposes for reading. The power lies in being able to recognise what kind of text is being read and select strategies and purposes with flexibility. To be a 'real' reader is to have power over what is being read rather than be at its mercy. 'Real' readers know how to read 'pulp fiction' and a 'literary novel'; they can choose to do both, either or neither. 'Real' readers know that reading is often hard work, demanding, challenging. In retrospect it can be rewarding but the process is not without effort. How did 'real' readers discover that it is worth making the effort? How can teachers help young readers to make that discovery for themselves?

There is still a lot we do not know about reading. We need to know more about what is happening when our pupils read 'pulp' fiction or watch television and video. The idea that these are 'passive activities' where 'nothing is happening' is not helpful to anyone hoping to create 'real' readers. We need to find out what readers (and viewers) are learning about reading (and viewing) from this material so that we can help them to learn to read a greater variety of texts; so that they can discover how screen story is different from (not necessarily better or worse than) print story; so that they can take on more demanding reading. This is not unrelated to the National Curriculum. The Cox report reminds us that 'questions of media education can be applied to literature' and, at best, we can look for a rich association of the two in English.

For teachers who want to create 'real' readers, the materials and information in *Reading Alive!* will be a useful tool. Teachers who have been looking at them with me can't wait to get their hands on them. Used with understanding, common sense and good instinct, they should give positive results. Used otherwise they could become number thirty-one on the list of Ways to Kill Reading.

It's up to you.

Pat Triggs

Thirty ways to kill reading

1 *Make sure no-one in your school has the chance to behave like a 'real' reader.*

2 Never give any precious class time to talking about books or authors.

3 Don't give pupils opportunities to talk about what they are reading.

4 Colour code books (or use some other method) so that everyone is aware of how 'good' or 'bad' they are at reading. Don't let anyone choose a book that is 'too easy' or 'too hard'.

5 Never join in talking about books except to ask 'Did you enjoy it? Why?'

6 Insist on a review or a written response to every book read.

7 Have library time every week and insist everyone takes out a book – don't worry about whether they ever read it.

8 Never give anyone time to read.

9 Make sure you 'do' comprehension regularly from text books.

10 Create an environment that discourages reading. Start by putting up a poster about books or authors and leave it there to gather dust, curl up at the edges, get torn and be ignored.

11 Keep the library locked or inaccessible at lunchtime and after school. Use it mostly for governors' meetings.

12 Make sure there is never anyone around the books to help or advise.

13 Let the teacher librarian dose the children with 'library skills' once a year and hope this acts as a slow release vitamin. Don't mention library skills at any other time.

14 Make sure the teacher librarian or librarian never communicates except about overdue books or eating in the library.

15 Don't give a teacher librarian time to do the job properly. (Preferably appoint someone who knows nothing about books or reading).

16 Don't devise any ways potential readers might find books they would enjoy. Never ask pupils to suggest books for school.

17 Shelve all books spine out.

18 Don't have books in classrooms. If you do, make sure that 'reading' books are given greater status than 'real' books.

19 Never discard books that are dirty, tattered, out-of-date; in fact, spend as little as possible on books.

20 Apart from books for 'learning to read' which everyone (especially remedial readers) need to stay 'on' until they have finished the scheme, behave as if books were unimportant; use worksheets, cards, reading laboratories, exercises etc. instead.

21 Never read aloud; if you do, never do it regularly, never finish the book you start reading, never read the book first yourself (unless it's the one you read last year and the year before and the year before that), never practise, never choose anything new.

22 Remember only infants have carpets and cushions in book corners. No one over eight should be able to find somewhere comfortable to read in school.

23 Have a Book Week once a year to raise funds for another computer. Don't prepare for it or follow it up.

24 Don't on any account open a school bookshop or organise a book club or hold a book swap.

25 Make it clear that comics, joke books, riddles, magazines, newspapers are not wanted in the classroom.

26 *Be a good non-reading model.*

27 Avoid reading in silent reading time – mark books or do some admin. – anything to indicate that there are more important things to do.

28 Don't read yourself because you don't have time. Who does?

29 Don't talk about books to your colleagues or to your pupils.

30 Don't try to keep up with what is being published for children; don't read reviews, join professional associations, go to meetings or attend courses.

And just three ways to create readers

Provide
1. **A reader friendly environment**
2. **Time to read and be read to**
3. **Time to talk about reading**

Which means . . .

A **Making accessible for reference, borrowing, browsing and buying, reading material of all kinds:** fiction, non-fiction, poetry, drama; and in all forms: magazines, comics, newspapers.

B **Having a school bookshop and/or book club,** run by parents, teachers and volunteers, preferably in co-operation.

C **Organising a book day or book week.** Prepare for this months in advance and follow up so that it is clear to everyone that reading development is the underlying aim of all this activity.

D **Involving readers in selection of books** for school, weeding stock, and promotion, putting up displays and organising book events. Give readers a say in what is going to happen, as well as letting them do the work.

E **Establishing reading identity.** Enabling children to see themselves as readers, encouraging them to behave like readers and to be aware of what readers do. Talking together about when and how and why we read: what we find easy or difficult, different purposes for reading, different styles of reading, different or favourite places to read. Teachers and librarians, or any experienced readers, can discuss their current reading: what they are finding relaxing, challenging but rewarding, difficult, boring, can't-put-it-down. (The questionnaire on page 57 could get you started.)

F **Making time for reading.** Stop feeling guilty about setting aside time for daily silent reading. Instigate USSR, ERIC – or any other acronym you like, provided it means that everyone stops and reads something of their own choice. Put a 'Do not Disturb/Reading in Progress' sign on the door. Provide support for those who find it difficult at first. Have lunch-time silent reading clubs.

G *Keeping reading logs.* These could be simple records of author, title and star rating, which are reviewed regularly with a knowledgeable reader who will listen, learn, question ('As a reader how did you find . . .?'), share ('I read something like that') and suggest ways forward ('If you want to extend your range you could try . . .'). You could also keep records of responses: a place to note down feelings, reactions, personal connections, questions. These may be private, or shared with the teacher or others who are reading the same book.

H *Reading aloud . . . daily.* Read variety: jokes, riddles, newspapers, articles, book and film reviews and letters, as well as stories, poetry, non-fiction books, including biography and autobiography. Read everything yourself before you read it aloud. Choose books to read aloud which you value – not just those you know will be instantly popular. Find ways to create a context for listening: agree ground rules about where and how listeners can sit: what is OK while listening (drawing? plaiting your friend's hair? knitting? eating and drinking?). Introduce the story: talk about why you chose it, what sort of story it is, recap the last episode. Don't be afraid to edit (in advance): select highlights, write linking summaries, tell your listeners what you have done and why, make the book available for those who want to read it all. Read openings: get listeners into the book and then leave them to go on individually. Discuss, compare, relish, repeat and re-write phrases and sentences that are striking or memorable – even clichés: Draw attention to language and the way it is used.

I *Increasing awareness of authors and titles.* Build up an author clipping file; readers, in pairs, could create an author file. Put up displays: author of the month, book of the month. Compile a fiction database. Involve readers in deciding on the categories they think will help them find the books they want to read and in deciding which books fit which category. Keep this up-to-date. Arrange an author visit with thorough preparation and follow up. Compile a class Top Twenty using suggestions from reading logs; promote discussion and voting, with cases for and against. Keep a file of authors' birthdays. Have 'weeks': poetry week, ghost story week. Use activities 41, 42, 43, and 45.

J *Extending the reading network.* Involve parents, friends and other interested readers with reading logs, shared reading, family reading groups and reading time, as well as helping in the library or school bookshop with book events. Write to other readers, editors, authors and publishers about matters of interest or concern.

K *Deepening and extending response.* Use activities which take the reader into the book rather than use it as a springboard. Select activities 29, 34, 35, 36, 37, 40, 44, 47 from *Reading Alive!* and invent your own.

Above all, remember that reading is a social activity. Provide opportunities for talking and sharing response, thinking aloud, asking questions, sharing connections or confusions, finding patterns, linking with other reading. Through everything you do in the classroom, make clear your conviction that you only learn to develop a variety of reading strategies by reading a variety of materials every day – and, that we never stop learning to read.

How to use the activities and lists

The activities

The activities (as well as the Student Questionnaire on p 57, and the Readership Award Certificate on p 59, are **free of copyright**, so that groups of readers can do the same activity with different books, or different activities based on the same book.

This is not a reading programme. The activities are intended to provide readers with a wide range of options for examining their response to some books. No child should be required to 'do' something every time he reads a book.

All the activities are designed to make it easier for children to share and extend their feelings and opinions about books; to provide a focus for their discussions. Talking can precede or follow the completion of an activity; readers can collaborate; activities can be done during or after reading. Most of the activities can be used across the 8–14 age range; where this is not so a note is included with the Book List. It is up to the teacher to create the climate and context in which children of all ages can exercise control and choice about their reading.

These activities are no substitute for teachers' involvement with and knowledge of books and the reading habits and preferences of their students. There can be no substitute for a teacher who loves books and reading.

The book lists

On the back of each activity is a list of appropriate books. Books are marked * if they are suitable for younger (8–10) or less experienced readers, and † if suitable for older (13–14) or more experienced readers. Please use these categories only as a guide and let your own knowledge of children as readers and people determine which titles to make available.

Books on the lists cover a wide range of reading development and competence. Included are titles to increase the range of competent and committed readers, sophisticated picture books and books to engage struggling and inexperienced readers.

The lists are a starting point for teachers. Don't give students the lists and say 'go and find one of these books and read it'. The lists are copyright to prevent this. Please look at the lists to check which are available to you; decide which ones are suitable; substitute and add.

The lists are grouped under Stories, Poetry and Picture Books where this seemed useful. Paperback editions are listed on the assumption that you may wish to purchase some of the titles. Hardback editions and out of print titles can be pursued in libraries. Publishing information was correct when the lists were compiled but the situation changes rapidly, so we advise checking.

The original book lists were Gwen Gawith's personal selection of 'the books I believe in, the books I'd like to see in every school library'. Pat Triggs has amended and expanded the lists for UK schools.

LISTEN TO THE WORDS ON THE PAGE!

and choose your favourite pieces for the empty balloons

Lie in a layabout, languorous laze,
Dreaming of dallying doze-around days.

MAHY, Margaret *The pirates mixed-up voyage* (Magnet)

When the darkness crowds beyond the door, and the logs on the hearth burn clear red and fall in upon themselves, making caverns and ships and swords and dragons and strange faces in the heart of the fire, that is the time for story telling.

SUTCLIFFE, Rosemary
The Road to Camlann (Knight)

'What king of pudding will you make!' Huey said.
'A wonderful pudding,' my father said. 'It will taste like a whole raft of lemons. It will taste like a night on the sea.'

CAMERON, Ann.
The Julian Stories
(Young Lions)

Listen to the Words on the Page

Here are books chosen for reading aloud because of the quality of the language. The list includes short and long stories, modern and traditional tales, myths, legends and folk tales, poetry and rhyme. The focus here is on words and the sound of words read aloud, but some of these titles come in picture book form so don't forget to encourage readers to enjoy and be aware of the different ways words and pictures combine.

STORIES

AIKEN, Joan   *Mortimer and the sword Excalibur,* ill. Quentin Blake (BBC)
    *Kingdom under the sea (Puffin)
    A necklace of raindrops, ill. Jan Pienkowski (Puffin)
* BISSET, Donald   *Upside down stories* (Young Puffin)
BOSTON, Lucy   *The children of Green Knowe* (Puffin) and other titles
* CAMERON, Ann   *The Julian stories* (Young Lions)
COLWELL, Eileen   *Various anthologies and collections* (Puffin)
DICKINSON, Peter   *City of gold,* ill. Michael Foreman, re-tellings of stories from The Bible (Gollancz)
ELKIN, Judith, ed.   *The new golden land anthology* (Puffin)
FLEISCHMANN, Sid   *Ghost in the noonday sun* (Puffin) and other titles
GARFIELD, Leon   *The apprentices* (Puffin)
    Shakespeare's stories, ill. Michael Foreman (Gollancz hb)
GARNER, Alan   *A book of British fairy tales* (Collins)
GRAHAME, Kenneth   *The reluctant dragon* (Collins Lions)
    The wind in the willows, ill. John Burningham (Puffin)
    The wind in the willows, ill. E.H. Shepherd (Magnet)
* HADLEY, Eric and Teresa   *Legends of earth, air, fire and water* (CUP)
IRESON, Barbara, ed.   *In a class of their own,* school stories (Puffin)
JAFFREY, Madhur   *Seasons of splendour* (Pavilion)
JONES, Terry   *Fairy tales,* ill. Michael Foreman (Puffin)
LANG, Andrew, ed.   B. Alderson *Blue fairy book* (Puffin Classics)
LAYTON, George   *The fib and other stores* (Collins Lions)
* LOBEL, Arnold   *Fables* (Cape)
    Frog and Toad are friends (Puffin) and other titles
MAHY, Margaret   **Jam: a true story* (Magnet)
    Chocolate porridge and other stories (Puffin) and other story collections
    †*The changeover* (Magnet) †*Memory* (Puffin Plus)
† MARK, Jan   *Feet and other stories* (Puffin Plus)
SALWAY, Lance, ed.   *Magnet book of spine chillers* (Magnet)
SUTCLIFF, Rosemary   *The light beyond the forest* (Knight)
    The Road to Camlann (Knight)
WILLIAMSON, Duncan   *Fireside tales of the traveller children* (Canongate)

POETRY

AHLBERG, Allan   *Please Mrs Butler* (Puffin)
CAUSLEY, Charles   *Figgie Hobbin* (Puffin)
    ed. *Puffin Book of magic verses* (Puffin)
* IRESON, Barbara, ed.   *Young Puffin book of verse* (Young Puffin)
* MILNE A.A.   *Now we are six* (Magnet)
McGOUGH, Roger   *Sky in the pie* (Puffin)
NICHOLS, Grace   *Come on into my tropical garden* (Black h/b)

PICTURE BOOKS

AARDEMA, Vera   *Bringing the rain to Kapiti plain,* traditional rhyming tale (Picturemac)
* BLAKE, Quentin   *Mr Magnolia,* simple rhyme (Picture Lions)
* DODD, Lynley   *Hairy Maclary from Donaldson's dairy,* rhyming tale (Picture Puffin)
* HUTCHINS, Pat   *Don't forget the bacon* (Picture Puffin)
KEEPING, Charles and CROSSLEY-HOLLAND, Kevin   *Beowulf* (OUP)
KEEPING, Charles and NOYES, Alfred   *The highwayman* (OUP)
LeCAIN, Errol and LONGFELLOW, Henry Wadsworth   *Hiawatha's childhood* (Picture Puffin)
* MAHY, Margaret and WILLIAMS, Jenny   *The lion in the meadow* (Picture Puffin)
McCLURE, Gillian and COLTMAN, Paul   *Tog the ribber – or Granny's tale,* poem (Deutsch hb op)

ALPHABETICAL AUTHORS

NAME _____

Every time you read a book, fill in the author's surname in the correct alphabetical book. Can you find any authors for Q and X and Z?

A AHLBERG, Janet and Allan
AIKEN, Joan
ALEXANDER, Lloyd
AMBRUS, Victor
ANNO, Mitsumasa
ASHLEY, Bernard

A

B

C

D

E

F

G

H

I

J

K

L

M

N

O

P

Q

R

S

T

U

V

W

X

Y

Z

If I read a new author every 2 weeks, I'll get through the alphabet this year

AUTHOR A-Z

MY FAVOURITE AUTHOR IN _____ WAS:
YEAR

_____

Alphabetical Authors

A

AHLBERG, Janet and Allan
AIKEN, Joan
ALEXANDER, Lloyd
AMBRUS, Victor
ANNO, Mitsumasa
ASHLEY, Bernard

B

BABBITT, Natalie
BAWDEN, Nina
BERRY, James
BLUME, Judy
BONSALL, Cosby
BRIGGS, Raymond
BROWNE, Anthony
BURNINGHAM, John
BYARS, Betsy

C

CATE, Dick
CHAMBERS, Aidan
CHRISTOPHER, John
CLEARY, Beverley
CRESSWELL, Helen
CROSS, Gillian

D

DAHL, Roald
DARKE, Marjorie
DAVIES, Andrew
DE JONG, Meindert
DICKINSON, Peter
DOHERTY, Berlie

E

EARNSHAW, Brian
EDWARDS, Dorothy
ESCOTT, John

F

FARMER, Penelope
FATCHEN, Max
FINE, Anne
FISK, Nicholas
FOREMAN, Michael
FOX, Paula
FRANZEN, Nils-Olof
FRENCH, Fiona

G

GARDAM, Jane
GARFIELD, Leon
GARNER, Alan
GAVIN, Jamila
GEE, Maurice
GERAS, Adele
GIFF, Patricia Reilly
GOBLE, Paul
GODDEN, Rumer
GOSCINNY, Rene
GRANT, Gwen

H

HARDCASTLE, Michael
HILL, Douglas
HINTON, Nigel
HOBAN, Russell
HOOVER, H.M.
HOWE, James
HOWKER, Janni
HUGHES, Monica
HUNTER, Mollie

I

IBBOTSON, Eva
IMPEY, Rose
IRESON, Barbara

J

JANSSON, Tove
JEFFERIES, Roderic
JONES, Diane Wynne
JONES, Terry

K

KAYE, Geraldine
KEEPING, Charles
KELLEHER, Victor
KEMP, Gene
KENNEMORE, Tim
KERR, M.E.
KING, Clive
KING-SMITH, Dick
KLEIN, Robin
KONIGSBURG, E.L.

L

LAVELLE, Sheila
LEESON, Robert
LE GUIN, Ursula
LEWIS, C.S.
LINDGREN, Astrid
LINE, David
LINGARD, Joan
LITTLE, Lean
LIVELY, Penelope
LOWRY, Lois

M

McBRATNEY, Sam
McCAUGHREAN, Geraldine
McCUTCHEON, Elsie
McKEE, David
McKINLEY, Robin
MAHY, Margaret
MANNING-SANDERS, Ruth
MARK, Jan
MAYNE, William
MORPURGO, Michael

N

NAIDOO, Beverley
NAUGHTON, Bill
NEEDLE, Jan
NORTON, Andre
NOSTLINGER, Christine

O

OAKLEY, Graham
O'BRIEN, Robert C.
O'DELL, Scott
OXENBURY, Helen

P

PALMER, C. Everard
PARK, Ruth
PATERSON, Katherine
PEARCE, Phillippa
PEET, Bill
PEYTON, K.M.
PHIPSON, Joan
PILLING, Ann
PREUSSLER, Otfried
PRICE, Susan
PROYSEN, Alf

R

RAYNER, Mary
RICHLER, Mordecai
ROBINSON, Barbara
ROCKWELL, Thomas
RODDA, Emily
RODGERS, Mary
ROSEN, Michael
ROSS, Tony

S

SEFTON, Catherine
SELDEN, George
SHERRY, Sylvia
SMITH, Joan
SOUTHALL, Ivan
SPIER, Peter
STEIG, William
STEVENSON, James
STORR, Catherine
STRONG, Jeremy
SUTCLIFF, Rosemary

T

THIELE, Colin
TOWNSEND, John Rowe
TULLY, John

U

UDERZO, Albert
UNGERER, Tomi
URE, Jean
UTTLEY, Alison

V

VAN ALLSBERG, Chris
VESTLEY, Ann-Cath
VIORST, Judith
VOIGT, Cynthia

W

WADDELL, Martin
WALSH, Jill Paton
WELLS, Rosemary
WESTALL, Robert
WHITE, E.B.
WHITE, T.H.
WILDER, Laura Ingalls
WILLIAMS, Jay
WILLIAMS, Ursula Moray
WRIGHTSON, Patricia

Y

YEOMAN, John
YOLEN, Jane

Z

ZABEL, Jennifer
ZEMACH, Margot
ZIEFERT, Harriet
ZINDEL, Paul
ZION, Gene
ZOLOTOW, Charlotte

word magic

Words you love to say softly, slowly, fast, loudly, silently, words you like to write, words you like to see, words . . .

Pugilistical
AHLBERG, Janet and Allan *Please Mrs Butler* (Puffin)

Mellifluously
MAHY, Margaret *The pirates mixed-up voyage* (Magnet)

Diddling
HOBAN, Russell *Dinner at Alberta's* (Puffin)

MAGIC WORD LIST

_____

Pugilistical
_____

Mellifluously
_____

Diddling
_____

_____

_____

_____

_____

_____

_____

_____

_____

Swap your list with friends. What were their words? Where did they come from?

Word Magic

These titles are suitable for all ages if they are introduced in the context of exploring and enjoying rich, imaginative, unusual language. Select and prepare extracts for reading aloud to get things going.

STORIES

AHLBERG, Janet and Allan   *Jeremiah in the dark woods* (Collins Lions)
The clothes horse (Puffin)
BERRY, James   *A thief in the village* (Puffin)
FLEISCHMANN, Sid   *McBroom's wonderful one-acre farm* (Puffin)
GARNER Alan   *The stone book* (Collins Lions)
Granny Reardun (Collins Lions)
The aimer gate (Collins Lions)
Tom Fobble's day (Collins Lions)
HOBAN, Russell   *Dinner at Alberta's* (Puffin)
The marzipan pig (Puffin)
HUGHES, Ted   *How the whale became and other stories* (Young Puffin)
HUNTER, Norman   *Count Backwerdz on the carpet and other incredible stories* (Puffin)
JANSSON, Tove   *Finn Family Moomintroll* and series (Puffin)
JUSTER, Norton   *The phantom tollbooth* (Collins Lions)
KIPLING, Rudyard   *Just so stories*, ill. Michael Foreman (Puffin)
LEESON, Robert   *Slambash wangs of a Compo Gorner* (Collins Lions)
LINDSAY, Norman   *The magic pudding* (Angus and Robertson op)
MAHY, Margaret   *Pirates' mixed up voyage* (Magnet)
The chewing gum rescue, short story collections (Magnet)
Great piratical rumbustification (Puffin)
MAUROIS, Andre   *Fattypuffs and Thinifers* (Puffin)
MAYNE, William   *Hob stories*, several titles (Walker pb)
THURBER, James   *Thirteen Clocks and The wonderful O* (Puffin)

POETRY

AGARD, John   *I din do nuttin* (Magnet)
Say it again Granny (Magnet)
CAUSLEY, Charles   *Figgie Hobbin* (Puffin)
EDWARDS, Richard   *The word party* (Young Puffin)
ELIOT, T.S.   *Old Possum's book of practical cats* (Faber)
HENRI, Adrian   *The phantom lollipop lady* (Magnet)
HUGHES, Ted   *Ffangs the vampire bat and the kiss of truth* (Faber hb)
McGOUGH, Roger   *Sky in the pie* (Puffin)
MILNE, A.A   *The king's breakfast* (Methuen)
MITCHELL, Adrian   *Nothingmas day* (Allison and Busby)
OWEN, Gareth   *Song of the City* (Collins Lions)
PLATH, Sylvia   *The bed book* (Faber)
ROSEN, Michael   *Hairy tales and nursery crimes* (Collins Lions)
Mind your own business (Collins Lions)
Wouldn't you like to know (Puffin)
Spollyollydiddlytiddlyitis (Walker)
Hard-boiled legs (Walker)
WRIGHT, Kit   *Rabbiting On* (Collins Lions)

PICTURE BOOKS

AGARD, John and KENNAWAY, Adrienne   *Lend me your wings* (Hodder)
ELIOT, T.S. and LeCAIN, Errol   *Growltiger's last stand and other poems* (Faber hb)
HOBAN, Russell and BLAKE Quentin   *How Tom beat Captain Najork and his hired sportsmen*,
b&w ills. (Cape hb; Pan Piper Flippers)
LEAR, Edward and OXENBURY Helen   *Quangle Wangle's Hat* (Picture Puffin)
ROSEN, Michael and BLAKE, Quentin   *You can't catch me* (Picture Puffin)
UNGERER, Tomi   *Zeralda's Ogre* (Magnet)

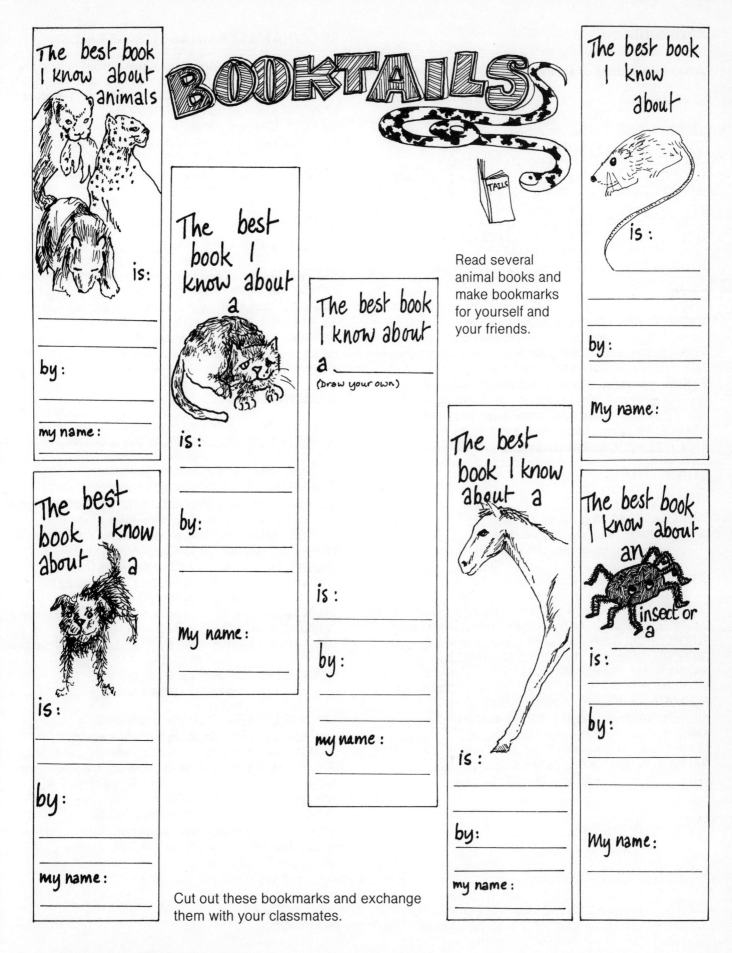

BOOKTAILS

The best book I know about animals

is: _____

by: _____

my name: _____

The best book I know about a

is: _____

by: _____

My name: _____

The best book I know about a _____
(Draw your own)

is: _____

by: _____

my name: _____

The best book I know about

is: _____

by: _____

My name: _____

The best book I know about a

is: _____

by: _____

my name: _____

The best book I know about an _____ **insect or a**

is: _____

by: _____

My name: _____

Read several animal books and make bookmarks for yourself and your friends.

Cut out these bookmarks and exchange them with your classmates.

Booktails

Well-known authors of animal stories include the following:

* BOND, Michael   *Olga da Polga, guinea pig stories* (Young Puffin)
  CORBETT, W.J.   *Pentecost series, a three book mouse quest* (Puffin)
  DANN, Colin   *The Farthing Wood* series (Sparrow)
  DeJONG, Meindert   Humans interacting with animals
* HERRIOT, James   Vet stories in picture books, various illustrators
  KING-SMITH, Dick   Zany animal romps (Puffin)
  KJELGAARD, Jim   Wild animal stories (Transworld, many titles op)
  STRANGER, Joyce   Realistic, accurate stories

CATS

* ARKLE, Phyllis   *The railway cat's secret,* and other titles (Young Puffin)
  ASHLEY, Bernard   *Calling for Sam* (Orchard Storybooks, Clipper St series)
  BAKER, Margaret   *Porterhouse Major* (Methuen)
* CASTOR, Harriet   *Fat Puss and friends* (Young Puffin)
* HOOKE, Nina Warner   *The snow kitten* (Young Puffin)
* PEARCE, Philippa   *Mrs Cockle's Cat* (Puffin)
* STOLZ, Mary   *Cat Walk* (Young Lions)

DOGS

  ATKINSON, Eleanor   *Greyfriars' Bobby* (Puffin)
* BERG, Leila   *My dog Sunday* (Puffin)
* BROWN, Ruth   *Our puppy's holiday* (Andersen, picture book) *Our cat Flossie* (Puffin)
  CRESSWELL, Helen   *Ordinary Jack* (Puffin) *Absolute zero* (Puffin)
* DUMAS, Philipe   *Laura, Alice's new puppy* (Young Lions)
  DeJONG, Meindert   *Hurry home Candy* (Collins Lions)
  FITZPATRICK, Sir Percy   *Jock of the Bushveld* (Puffin)
  GIFFORD, Griselda   *Because of Blunder* (Gollancz)
* HARRIOT, Ted and KOPPER, Lisa   *Coming home* (Lynx, picture book)
* HOOKE, Nina Warner   *Little dog lost* (Puffin)
  KILNER, Geoffrey   *Jet, a gift to the family* (Puffin)
  KNIGHT, Eric   *Lassie come home* (Puffin)
* MUIR, Frank   *What-a-mess,* various stories (Picture Corgi)
  NAUGHTON, Bill   *A dog called Nelson* (Puffin) See also *My pal Spadger*

MICE/HAMSTERS/RABBITS/GERBILS

† ADAMS, Richard   *Watership Down* (Puffin)
  BANKS, Lynne Reid   *Houdini: the story of a self-educated hamster* (Dragon)
  LAWSON, Robert   *Rabbit Hill* (Puffin)
  OAKLEY, Graham   *The church mice series* (Picturemac)
  O'BRIEN, Robert C.   *Mrs Frisby and the rats of NIMH* (Collins Lions)
  PEARCE, Philippa   *The battle of Bubble and Squeak* (Puffin)

HORSES

  COOKSON, Catherine   *The nipper* (Puffin) *Joe and the gladiator* (Puffin)
  FARLEY, Walter   *The black stallion* (Knight) and series
  FIDLER, Kathleen   *Haki, the Shetland pony* (Kelpie)
  GARDAM, Jane   *Bridget and William* (Young Puffin)
  MORPURGO, Michael   *Warhorse* (Magnet)
† PEYTON, K.M.   *Fly-by-night* (OUP)
  SEWELL, Anna   *Black Beauty* (Puffin)
  STEINBECK, John   *The red pony* (Pan Piper)

GENERAL

  BAWDEN, Nina   *Keeping Henry* (Puffin) squirrel
† BURNFORD, Sheila   *The incredible journey* (Hodder Coronet)
  BYARS, Betsy   *The midnight fox* (Puffin)
  CHAMBERS, Aidan   *Seal Secret* (Hippo)
  CORRIN, Sarah and Stephen   *Puffin book of pet stories* (Puffin)
  CUNLIFFE, John   *Small monkey tales* (Puffin)
  DeJONG, Meindert   *Wheel on the school* (Puffin) storks
  DERWENT, Lavinia   *Sula* (Cannongate) seal
  DILLON, Eilis   *A family of foxes* (Puffin)
  HARVEY, Ann ed.   *Of caterpillars, cats and cattle* poetry (Puffin)
  IRESON, Barbara ed.   *Creepy-crawly stories* (Beaver)
  JENKINS, Alan   *The ghost elephant* (Puffin)
  KENEALLY, Thomas   *Ned Kelly and the city of the bees* (Puffin)
  KEMP, Gene   *Dog days and cat naps* short story collection (Puffin)
  MAXWELL, Gavin   *The otter's tale* (Puffin)
* MORGAN, Alison   *Bright-eye* (Puffin) wild duck
  MORPURGO, Michael   *When the whales came* (Magnet)
† RAWLINGS, Marjorie Kinnan   *The yearling* (Pan Piper)
  SCHOLES, Katherine   *The boy and the whale* (Puffin)
  SELDEN, George   *The cricket in Times Square* and other titles (Puffin)
  WAHL, Jan   *Pleasant Fieldmouse* (Puffin)
† WILLIAMSON, Henry   *Tarka the Otter* (Puffin)

teleletter

BREVITY IS THE SOUL OF WIT... AND SELLING

Choose a book with plenty of action. Take one really exciting incident and send a TELELETTER to a friend. You may use no more than 30 words. Here is an example: Boy overhears murder plot (stop) Finds own life in danger (stop) (*Run for Your Life*, by David Line). Don't try to tell the whole plot ... just one incident which will be interesting enough to make your friend want to read the book.

Fold the TELELETTER in three and write your friend's name on the outside.

WRITE NAME OF FRIEND ON BACK WHEN YOU HAVE FOLDED IT...

AUTHOR _____

TITLE _____

Ⓐ (FOLD Ⓐ SO THAT TIP OF ENVELOPE SLIDES INTO SLOT) ....

_____

_____

_____

_____

_____

WORD COUNT_____ (DO NOT COUNT 'STOP')   (MAXIMUM 30 WORDS)

Ⓑ ....

FROM: _____

CUT HERE   SLOT

Ⓒ (FOLD ALONG Ⓑ SO THAT Ⓒ MEETS Ⓐ)

Teleletter

This activity is quite a challenge: it focuses and develops selection and summarising. Working in pairs is useful for beginners.

* AHLBERG, Janet and Allan   *Burglar Bill* (Picture Lions)
The vanishment of Thomas Tull (Puffin)
AIKEN, Joan   *The whispering mountain* (Puffin) and other titles
* ASHLEY, Bernard   *A bit of give and take* (Young Corgi)
† BISCHOFF, David   *Wargames* (Puffin Plus)
* BROWN, Jeff   *Flat Stanley* (Magnet)
CHAMBERS, Aidan   *The present takers* (Magnet)
CHEETHAM, Ann   *Black harvest* (Armada)
COOPER, Susan   *Over sea, under stone* (Puffin)
CROSS, Gillian   *The runaway* (Magnet)
Strike at Ratchliffe's Rags (Magnet)
DAHL, Roald   *The BFG* (Puffin)
DAVIES, Andrew   *Alfonso Bonzo* (Magnet)
DAVIES, Hunter   Flossie Teacake series (Young Lions)
Oswald Osgood (Ossie) series (Young Lions)
De HAMEL, Joan   *X marks the spot* (Puffin)
FISK, Nicholas   *Antigrav* (Puffin)
Grinny (Puffin)
Robot revolt (Puffin)
Timetrap (Puffin)
GEE, Maurice   *Under the mountain* (Puffin) and other titles
HARRISON, Harry   *The men from P.I.G. and R.O.B.O.T.* (Puffin)
* HEIDE, Florence Parry   *The shrinking of Treehorn* (Puffin)
HINTON, Nigel   *Beaver Towers* (Knight)
The Witch's Revenge (Knight)
HUGHES, Monica   *Sandwriter* (Magnet) and other SF titles
* HUGHES, Shirley   *Chips and Jessie* (Young Lions)
HUTCHINS, Pat   *The curse of the Egyptian mummy* (Collins Lions)
* LAVELLE, Sheila   *Ursula camping* (Young Corgi) and other titles
LINDGREN, Astrid   *Emil in the soup tureen* (Beaver) and other titles
LINE, David   *Run for your life* (Puffin) and other titles
MACKEN, Walter   *Island of the great yellow ox* (Piper)
McBRATNEY, Sam   *Zesty* (Magnet) and other titles
O'BRIEN Robert   *Mrs Frisby and the rats of NIMH* (Puffin)
* PHIPSON, Joan   *Hide till daytime* (Young Puffin)
PEYTON, K.M.   *Who, Sir? Me, Sir?* (Puffin)
PILLING, Ann   *The year of the worm* (Puffin)
Henry's Leg (Puffin)
POWLING, Chris   *Daredevils or scaredycats* (Collins Lions)
RICHLER, Mordecai   *Jacob Two-two meets the hooded fang* (Puffin)
SEFTON, Catherine   *Emer's ghost* (Magnet)
The ghost and Bertie Boggin (Puffin)
SERRAILLIER, Ian   *There's no escape* (Puffin)
SHERRY, Sylvia   *A pair of Jesus boots* (Puffin)
† SWINDELLS, Robert   *A Serpent's Tooth* (Puffin Plus)
* WILLIAMS, Ursula Moray   *The adventures of the little wooden horse* (Puffin)
WILSON, Bob   *Stanley Bagshaw and the twenty-two ton whale* (Picture Puffin)
WILSON, David Henry   *The fastest gun alive . . .* (Piper)
† WRIGHTSON, Patricia   *A little fear* (Puffin)

NAME OF DETECTIVE _____

Read a book with plenty of action and write it up as a detective's case study.

PLOT?
MOTIVE?
STYLE?

Ooo

AUTHOR _____ TITLE _____

DETECTIVE GAME

CASE STUDY

WHO? (The protagonists, main characters, villains, victims, heroines, heroes)

_____

_____

_____

WHAT happened? To whom? WHEN? HOW?

_____

_____

_____

_____

_____

WHERE? Place; location; country? Did it have any influence on what happened?

_____

_____

WHY? For what reason? Motives? Causes? Explanations? Evidence? Factors?

_____

_____

_____

So? With what result? Conclusion? What happened in the end? OK?

_____

_____

Detective Game

SERIES – including interactive and game books

BLIESENER, Klaus   *The ghostly break-in* (Magnet) interactive
* COREN, Alan   *Arthur, schoolboy detective* (Puffin)
DICKS, Terrance   *Baker St. Irregulars* (Magnet)
DIXON, Franklin W.   *Hardy Boys* (Armada)
ECKE, Wolfgang   *Super Sleuth books* (Magnet) interactive
* ESCOTT, John   *Roundbay Radio mysteries* (Young Puffin)
FRANZEN, Nils-Olof   *Agaton-Sax* (Deutsch)
HERGE   *Tintin* (Methuen)
HITCHCOCK, Alfred   *Three Investigators* (Armada)
KEENE, Carolyn   *Nancy drew* (Armada)
PRESS, Hans Jurgen   *The adventures of the Black Hand Gang* (Magnet) interactive

SINGLE TITLES

ASHLEY, Bernard   *Terry on the fence* (Puffin) and other titles
BAWDEN, Nina   *Kept in the dark* (Puffin)
BERESFORD, Elisabeth   *The mysterious island* (Magnet)
BERNA, Paul   *A hundred million francs* (Puffin)
CROSS, Gillian   *The mintyglo kid* (Magnet)
    The dark behind the curtain (Hippo)
    On the edge (Puffin)
    The runaway (Magnet)
† DUNCAN, Lois   *Locked in time* (Puffin Plus)
FISK, Nicholas   *Antigrav* (Puffin)
    Grinny (Puffin)
    Wheelie in the stars (Puffin)
GARFIELD, Leon   *The December Rose* (Puffin) and other titles
* HUGHES, Shirley   *It's too frightening for me* (Puffin)
HUTCHINS, Pat   *The Mona Lisa Mystery* (Young Lions)
† HINTON, Nigel   *Collision course* (Puffin)
KING, Clive   *Me and my millions* (Puffin)
    The sound of propellers (Puffin)
KING-SMITH, Dick   *The fox busters* (Puffin)
KLEIN, Robin   **Thingnapped* (OUP)
    Halfway across the galaxy and turn left (Puffin)
    People might hear you (Puffin)
LINE, David   *Run for your life* (Puffin)
MARKS, J.M.   *Hijacked* (Puffin)
PEYTON, K. M.   *A midsummer night's death* (Puffin Plus)
* PHIPSON, Joan   *Hide till daytime* (Puffin)
† RASKIN, Ellen   *The tattooed potato and other stories* (Puffin Plus)
WESTALL, Robert   *The machine gunners* (Puffin)
    † *The Watch House* (Puffin Plus)

YOUR NAME: _____

AUTHOR: _____

TITLE: _____

READING AS FEELING

DEPRESSED HOLLOW CURIOUS CONTENTED BETRAYED DISGUSTED ANXIOUS
VULNERABLE INTRIGUED OVERJOYED CONFUSED UPSET BAFFLED BITTER
ELATED PROUD DELIGHTED AMUSED RELIEVED WILD
FULFILLED HAPPY DISAPPOINTED CROSS
DISMAYED INVOLVED SAD BEWILDERED DEJECTED
SATISFIED ANGRY DETACHED
DISTRESSED FURIOUS
ANGUISHED ALONE
CALM PLEASED INDIGNANT
DEFENCELESS HURT MAD
DISPIRITED SCEPTICAL DISTRAUGHT INDIGNANT LONELY

When you've read your book, think about what you felt

I felt .... when ....

....

....

I felt .... when ....

....

....

I felt .... when ....

....

....

I felt .... when ....

....

....

....

I felt .... when ....

....

....

Reading as Feeling

If you are introducing response logs or journals to readers of any age, this activity will help you get started. The faces sketched on the sheet have deliberately ambiguous expressions to indicate that our responses as readers are rarely as obvious as 'happy' or 'sad'. There is opportunity here for teachers to help readers discover a wonderful range of 'feelings words'. Your own knowledge of the needs and abilities of the readers in your class will enable you to decide how much to intervene and – for instance – whether to adapt the activity and encourage recording responses at stages during the reading rather than all at the end. The Reading is feeling activity (p. 41) explores similar ground; older readers may prefer it.

STORIES

ANDERSON, Rachel   *The poacher's son* (Collins Lions)
ASHLEY, Bernard   *Calling for Sam* (Orchard Books)
Taller than before (Orchard Books)
Dinner ladies don't count (Young Puffin); *Break in the sun* (Puffin); *Running Scared* (Puffin Plus)
ATKINSON, Eleanor   *Greyfriar's Bobby* (Puffin)
BAWDEN, Nina   *The peppermint pig* (Puffin)
BLUME, Judy   *Freckle juice* (Heinemann Banana Books); *Superfudge; Tales of a fourth grade nothing* (both Piper)
BYARS, Betsy   *The house of wings; Summer of the swans; The Cybil war* (all Puffin) and other titles
CHAMBERS, Aidan   *Seal secret* (Hippo); *The present takers* (Magnet)
CRESSWELL, Helen   *The piemakers* (Puffin)
DAHL, Roald   *Danny the champion of the world* (Puffin)
* DALGLEISH, Alice   *The bears on Hemlock Mountain* (Young Puffin)
† DESAI, Anita   *The village by the sea* (Puffin Plus)
DICKINSON, Peter   *The devil's children* (Puffin)
* FARMER, Penelope   *Saturday by Seven* (Young Puffin); *The summer birds* (Bodley Bookshelf)
FINE, Anne   *Madame Doubtfire* (Puffin Plus)
GARDAM, Jane   *Bridget and William/Horse* (Young Puffin); *Kit in Boots* (Puffin)
GODDEN, Rumer   *The diddakoi* (Puffin); *The story of Holly and Ivy* (Young Puffin);
Tottie; the story of a dolls' house (Young Puffin)
HANN, Mary Downing   *The Sara summer* (Collins Lions)
* HOOKE, Nina Warner   *Little dog lost; The snow kitten* (both Young Puffins)
JONES, Diana Wynne   *Dogsbody* (Magnet Teens)
KAYE, Geraldine   *Comfort herself* (Magnet)
* LEAF, Munro   *The story of Ferdinand* (Puffin)
LINGARD, Joan   *The twelfth day of July; Frying as usual* (both Puffin)
† LIVELY, Penelope   *Going Back* (Puffin)
MAGORIAN, Michelle   *Goodnight Mr Tom* (Puffin)
NICHOLS, Grace   *Leslyn in London* (Hodder & Stoughton)
RODDA, Emily   *Something special* (Puffin)
† STRACHAN, Ian   *Journey of 1000 miles* (Magnet)
TOMLINSON, Jill   *The owl who was afraid of the dark* (Young Puffin)

PICTURE BOOKS

BROWNE, Anthony   *Gorilla* (Magnet)
BROWNE, Anthony and McAFEE, Annalena   *Kirsty knows best* (Magnet)
* DePAOLA, Tomie   *Nana upstairs and Nana downstairs; Oliver Button is a sissy* (both Magnet)
FOREMAN, Michael   *Dinosaurs and all that rubbish* (Picture Puffin)
GOBLE, Paul   *The girl who loved wild horses* (Picturemac)
* ORAM, Hiawyn and KITAMURA, Satoshi   *Angry Arthur; In the Attic* (both Picture Puffin)
SENDAK, Maurice   *Where the wild things are; Outside over there* (both Picture Puffin)
* SMITH, Miriam   *Kimi and the watermelon* (Picture Puffin)
WAGNER, Jenny and Brooks, Ron   *John Brown, Rose and the midnight cat* (Picture Puffin)

PREDICTIONS:PREDICTION

YOUR NAME: _____

AUTHOR: _____

TITLE: _____

READ THE FIRST CHAPTER, THEN STOP!

What do you think is going to happen? _____

_____

_____

Who are the main characters? _____

_____

What are they like? _____

_____

_____

_____

Do you feel caught up with the story and characters already?   Why?   Why not?

_____

_____

_____

Is there a main problem in the story . . . something the main character is going to have to overcome/come to grips with? How will he/she do it? _____

_____

_____

_____

_____

NOW FINISH THE BOOK

Were your predictions right?   Why/How? _____

_____

_____

_____

_____

_____

_____

_____

Predictions

ALCOCK, Vivien   *Travellers by night* (Collins Lions) and other titles
ASHLEY, Bernard   *Running scared* (Puffin) and other titles
BAILLIE, Allan   *Adrift* (Magnet)
BANKS, Lynne Reid   *The Indian in the cupboard* (Granada Dragon) and sequel
CHEETHAM, Ann   *The black harvest* (Armada)
DICKINSON, Peter   *The devil's children* (Puffin)
DOHERTY, Berlie   *Children of winter* (Collins Lions)
* FARMER, Penelope   *Saturday by seven* (Puffin)
* FEAGLES, Anita   *Casey the utterly impossible horse* (Puffin)
FOX, Paula   *The one-eyed cat* (Pan Piper)
* GARDAM, Jane   *Bridget and William/Horse* (Young Puffin)
GEE, Maurice   *Under the mountain* (Puffin)
† GILMORE, Kate   *Of griffins and graffiti* (Puffin Plus)
* GRAHAME, Kenneth   *The reluctant dragon* (Young Puffin)
HENTOFF, Nat   *Does this school have capital punishment?* (Piper)
† HINTON, Nigel   *Collision course* (Puffin)
                 Beaver Towers (Knight)
HOROWITZ, Anthony   *The night of the scorpion* (Magnet)
HOWE, James and Deborah   *Bunnicula* (Young Lions)
HUGHES, Monica   *Devil on my back* (Magnet) and other titles
JONES, Diana Wynne   *Archer's goon* (Magnet)
                 Homeward bounders (Magnet)
                 Magicians of Caprona (Beaver) and other titles
KING-SMITH, Dick   *Saddlebottom* (Puffin) and other titles
KLEIN, Robin   *People might hear you* (Puffin)
* LEE, Robert   *Microfish* (Magnet)
LIVELY, Penelope   *The ghost of Thomas Kempe* (Puffin)
MAHY, Margaret   *Clancy's cabin* (Puffin)
                 The great piratical rumbustification (Puffin)
                 †*The changeover* (Magnet Teens)
                 †*The haunting* (Magnet)
                 †*The tricksters* (Puffin Plus)
MARK, Jan   *Handles* (Puffin)
MATTINGLEY, Christine   *New patches for old* (Puffin)
MAYNE, William   *Kelpie* (Puffin)
O'SHEA, Pat   *The hounds of Morrigan* (Puffin)
* PHIPSON, Joan   *Hide till daytime* (Puffin)
POTTER, Margaret   *The boys who disappeared* (Puffin)
POWLING, Chris   *Mog and the Rectifier* (Knight)
RODGERS, Mary   *Freaky Friday* (Puffin)
† SCHLEE, Ann   *The vandal* (Magnet)
* SEFTON, Catherine   *The Emma dilemma* (Magnet) and other titles
SWINDELLS, Robert   *The ice palace* (Collins Lions)
                 †*Brother in the land* (Puffin Plus)
* TOWNSON, Hazel   *The shrieking face* (Beaver)
* WADDELL, Martin   *Harriet and the haunted school* (Hippo)
WAKEFIELD, S.A.   *Bottersnikes and Gumbles* (Young Piper) and series
† WESTALL, Robert   *The cats of Seroster* (Piper)
*WILSON, Gage   *Mrs Gaddy and the ghost* (Hippo)
WISEMAN, David   *The fate of Jeremy Visick* (Puffin)
YEOMAN, John and BLAKE, Quentin   *The boy who sprouted antlers* (Young Lions)

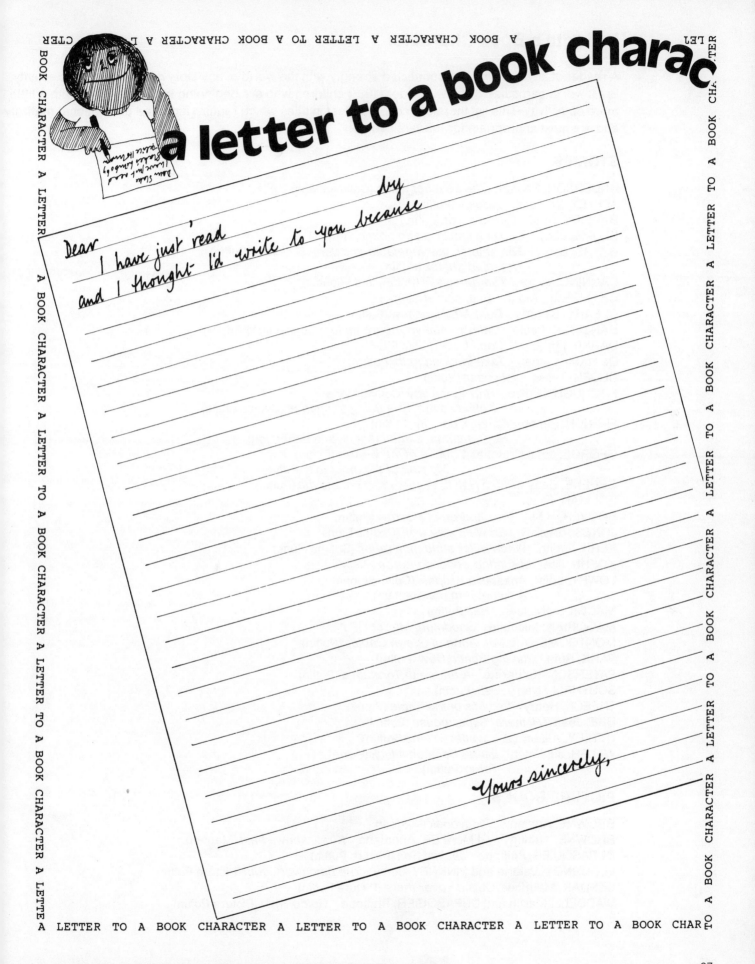

a letter to a book charac

Dear ,

I have just read *dry*

and I thought I'd write to you because

Yours sincerely,

Letter to a Book Character

A reader of any age who has connected strongly with the world of any story could choose this activity. But it works particularly well with older (10+) children who are beginning to see the world with a little more objectivity. This list therefore concentrates on titles which require a degree of emotional maturity and are most appropriate for readers over ten.

STORIES

ANDERSON, Rachel   *The poacher's son* (Collins Lions)
† ASHLEY, Bernard   *Dodgem* (Puffin)
BAWDEN, Nina   *Carrie's war* (Puffin)
BLUME, Judy   *Tale of a fourth grade nothing* (Piper)
BYARS, Betsy   *The animal, the vegetable and John D. Jones* (Puffin)
   The midnight fox (Puffin)
CANNING, Victor   *The runaways* (Puffin) and sequels
CHAMBERS, Aidan   *Seal secret* (Hippo)
CLEARY, Beverly   *Dear Mr. Henshaw* (Puffin)
DANZIGER, Paula   *Can you sue your parents for malpractice?* (Piper)
DARKE, Marjorie   *Comeback* (Puffin Plus)
De HAMEL, Joan   *Take the long path* (Puffin)
DUDER, Tessa   *Jellybean* (Puffin)
FITZHUGH, Louise   *Harriet the spy* (Collins Lions)
   Nobody's family is going to change (Collins Lions)
FRENCH, Simon   *Cannily, cannily* (Puffin)
   Hey, phantom singlet (Angus and Robertson)
GEORGE, Jean Craighead   *Julie of the wolves* (Puffin)
   My side of the mountain (Puffin)
GREENE, Betty   *Philip Hall likes me, I reckon, maybe* (Puffin)
HOLMAN, Felice   *Slake's limbo* (Collins Teen Tracks)
HOOVER, H.M.   *The children of Morrow* (Puffin)
JONES, Toeckey   *Go well, stay well* (Collins Lions)
KERR, Judith   *When Hitler stole pink rabbit* (Collins Lions)
† KOEHN, Ilse   *Mischling, second degree* (Puffin Plus)
LOWRY, Lois   *Anastasia Krupnik* (Collins Lions)
   A summer to die (Bantam)
MACGIBBON, Jean   *Hal* (Puffin)
MAGORIAN, Michelle   *Goodnight Mr Tom* (Puffin)
MONTGOMERY, L.M.   *Anne of Green Gables* (Puffin)
PARK, Ruth   *Playing Beatie Bow* (Puffin)
PATERSON, Katherine   *A bridge to Terabithia* (Puffin)
SOUTHALL, Ivan   *Josh* (Puffin)
TREECE, Henry   *Legions of the Eagle* (Puffin)
URE, Jean   *Hi there, Supermouse* (Puffin)
UTTLEY, Alison   *A traveller in time* (Puffin)
WALSH, Jill Paton   *Gaffer Samson's luck* (Puffin)
   Torch (Puffin)

PICTURE BOOKS

BROWNE, Anthony   *Piggybook* (Magnet)
BROWNE, Anthony and McAFEE, Annalena   *Kirsty knows best* (Magnet)
DUPASQUIER, Philippe   *Jack at Sea* (Picture Puffin)
FLOURNOY, Valerie and PINKNEY, Jerry   *The patchwork quilt* (Picture Puffin)
SENDAK, Maurice   *Outside over there* (Picture Puffin)
WADDELL, Martin and DUPASQUIER, Philippe   *Going West* (Picture Puffin)

emotion trail

YOUR NAME: _____

AUTHOR: _____

TITLE: _____

When you have read your book, work out the main events in the story (the plot) for Column 1, what the main character felt like during these events (the emotional plot) for Column 2, and what **you** felt like for Column 3.

1 PLOT (WHAT HAPPENED)	2 MAIN CHARACTER: HOW SHE/HE FELT	3 WHAT YOU FELT LIKE READING ABOUT IT

Did this book say anything to you about your own life and emotions? Your family? Your friends? Your own character and personality?

_____

_____

_____

Emotion Trail

An activity for all ages and stages. For developing readers it offers a useful framework for recording responses after group discussion.

STORIES

ASHLEY, Bernard   †*Janey* (Puffin Plus) and other titles
                            A bit of give and take (Young Corgi)
                            Dinner ladies don't count; I'm trying to tell you (both Young Puffin)
* CATE, Dick   *Old dog, new tricks* (Young Puffin)
CROSSLEY-HOLLAND, Kevin   *Storm* (Banana Books)
FOX, Paula   *One-eyed cat* (Piper)
* GARDAM, Jane   *Bridget and William/Horse* (Young Puffin)
HOWKER, Janni   *Badger on the barge* (Collins Lions) short stories
                         Isaac Campion; The nature of the beast (both Collins Lions)
HONES, Toeckey   *Go well, stay well* (Collins Lions)
KING-SMITH, Dick   *E.S.P.* (Young Corgi)
KLEIN, Robin   *Games; Hating Alison Ashby; People might hear you* (all Puffin)
† KOEHN, Ilse   *Mischling, second degree* (Puffin Plus)
KNIGHT, Eric   *Lassie come home* (Puffin)
MACLACHLAN, Patricia   *Sarah plain and tall* (Puffin)
† MAHY, Margaret   *Memory* (Puffin Plus)
                       Catalogue of the universe (Magnet)
† MARSHALL, James Vance   *Walkabout* (Puffin)
MATTINGLEY, Christobel   *The miracle tree* (Hodder & Stoughton)
                            Duck Boy (Young Puffin)
† MAYNE, William   *Drift* (Puffin)
* MORGAN, Alison   *Bright-eye* (Young Puffin)
NAIDOO, Beverley   *Journey to Jo'burg* (Young Lions)
NAUGHTON, Bill   *A dog called Nelson* (Puffin)
O'BRIEN, Robert   *Z for Zachariah* (Collins Lions)
PATERSON, Katherine   *A bridge to Terabithia* (Puffin)
PEARCE, Phillipa   *A dog so small* (Puffin)
                    What the neighbours did (Puffin) short stories
                    The way to Sattin shore (Puffin)
PEYTON, K.M.   *Prove yourself a hero* (Puffin Plus)
                  Who, Sir, Me Sir? (Puffin)
               †*A midsummer night's death* (Puffin Plus)
PULLMAN, Philip   *The ruby in the smoke* (Puffin) and sequels
* SMITH, Alexander McCall   *The perfect hamburger* (Young Puffin)
SMUCKER, Barbara   *Amish adventure* (Puffin)
                       Underground to Canada (Puffin)
† STRACHAN, Ian   *Moses Beech* (Puffin Plus)
† URE, Jean   *One green leaf* (Corgi Freeway)
                See you Thursday (Puffin Plus)
† VOIGT, Cynthia   *Homecoming* (Collins Lions) and sequels
WHEATLEY, Nadia   *The blooding* (Puffin Plus)
YOUNG, Helen   *What difference does it make, Danny?* (Young Lions)

PICTURE BOOKS

KINMONT, Patrick and CARTWRIGHT, Reg   *Mr Potter's pigeon* (Pocket Puffin)
* MARTIN, Bill   *The ghost-eye tree* (Picture Puffin)
* ORAM, Hiawyn and KITAMURA, Satoshi   *Angry Arthur* (Picture Puffin)
* SENDAK, Maurice   *Where the wild things are* (Picture Puffin)
* WADDELL, Martin and DUPASQUIER Philippe   *Going West* (Picture Puffin)

YOUR NAME _____

AUTHOR _____

TITLE _____

BETWEEN THE LINES AND BEHIND THE LINES

WHAT DO YOU THINK THE AUTHOR WAS TRYING TO SAY TO YOU?

_____
_____
_____
_____
_____
_____

DID THE AUTHOR, THROUGH THE STORY, MANAGE TO TELL YOU ANYTHING ABOUT YOURSELF THAT YOU HAD NOT THOUGHT ABOUT BEFORE?

_____
_____
_____
_____
_____
_____

WHAT SORT OF PERSON DO YOU THINK THE AUTHOR MUST BE TO WRITE A BOOK LIKE THIS?
Young / old / kind / nice / caring / friendly / understanding / lonely / miserable / unhappy / sensitive / knows what young people think and feel / out of touch / full of laughter

_____
_____
_____
_____
_____
_____

Between the Lines and Behind the Lines

STORIES

ANDERSON, Rachel   *The war orphan* (Swallow)
ASHLEY, Bernard   *A kind of wild justice* (Puffin)
* AVERY, Gillian   *Mouldy's orphan* (Young Puffin)
BLUME, Judy   *Deenie* (Piper)
BYARS, Betsy   *The eighteenth emergency* (Puffin)
        The pinballs (Puffin)
CHAMBERS, Aidan   *Seal Secret* (Hippo)
CORBETT, W.J.   *Pentecost and the chosen one* (Puffin)
† CORMIER, Robert   *The chocolate war* (Collins Teen Tracks)
* DAVIES, Evelyn   *Joseph's bear* (Young Puffin)
DE HORA, Luis   *The king who learned how to make friends* (Andersen hb)
DE JONG, Meindert   *The wheel on the school* (Puffin)
† DOHERTY, Berlie   *Granny was a buffer girl* (Collins Teen Tracks)
        White Peak Farm (Collins Teen Tracks)
FINE, Anne   *The Granny project* (Magnet)
FRENCH, Simon   *Cannily, cannily* (Puffin)
† GARNER, Alan   *The owl service* (Collins Teen Tracks)
† HUNTER, Mollie   *I'll go my own way* (Collins Teen Tracks)
HEIDE, Florence Parry   *The shrinking of Treehorn* (Puffin)
KAYE, Geraldine   *Comfort herself* (Magnet)
KEMP, Gene   *The turbulent term of Tyke Tiler* (Puffin)
KENNEMORE, Tim   *Wall of words* (Puffin)
KLEIN, Robin   *Boss of the pool* (Puffin)
        Penny Pollard's diary (OUP)
LINGARD, Joan   *The freedom machine* (Puffin)
        Frying as usual (Puffin)
† MAYNE, William   *Drift* (Puffin)
* NASH, Margaret   *Rat Saturday* (Young Puffin)
PEARCE, Philippa   *The battle of Bubble and Squeak* (Puffin)
        A dog so small (Puffin)
PILLING, Ann   *The year of the worm* (Puffin)
RODGERS, Mary   *Freaky Friday* (Puffin)
        Summer switch (Puffin)
* SHARMAT, Marjorie W.   *Mooch the messy* (Puffin)
† SWINDELLS, Robert   *Brother in the land* (Puffin Plus)
WALSH, Jill Paton   *Chance child; Dolphin crossing; Gaffer Sampson's luck* (all Puffin)

PICTURE BOOKS

BROWNE, Anthony   *A walk in the park* (Picturemac)
        Willy the wimp; Willy the champ (Magnet)
        Piggybook (Magnet)
* FOREMAN, Michael   *War and peas* (Picture Puffin)
        Dinosaurs and all that rubbish (Picture Puffin)
        Moose (Picture Puffin)
* LIONNI, Leo   *Fish is fish* (Picture Puffin)
MCKEE, David   **Not now Bernard* (Sparrow)
        The Admirals (Pocket Puffin)
        Snow woman (Andersen hb)
WAGNER, Jenny and Brooks, Ron   *John Brown, Rose and the midnight cat* (Picture Puffin)
* WILDE, Oscar and FOREMAN, Michael   *The selfish giant* (Picture Puffin)
* YEOMAN, John and BLAKE, Quentin   *The wild washerwomen* (Picture Puffin)

TAKING THE TEMPERATURE OF A BOOK

Blisfully Hot

NO GO BORED

NAME _____

AUTHOR _____

TITLE _____
_____

EMOTIONAL THERMOMETER

OVER THE TOP !

10
9
8
7
6
5
4
3
2
1

When you read this book how did you, as the reader, feel? Rate the book on the 0–10 thermometer scale (below) and try to explain why (opposite).

HOT

LUKEWARM

COLD

NO GO

My emotions ran really high. I couldn't put it down, I didn't want it to end because

_____
_____
_____
_____

I thought it was good but I couldn't get all steamed up about it because

_____
_____
_____
_____

I felt that I wanted to finish it but it was a bit of an effort because

_____
_____
_____

I only got to page _____ and didn't go on because

_____
_____
_____
_____

Taking the Temperature of a Book

STORIES

BANKS, Lynne Reid   *The Indian in the cupboard* (Dragon)
BAWDEN, Nina   *The peppermint pig* (Puffin)
* BERG, Leila   *My dog Sunday* (Young Puffin)
BYARS, Betsy   *The midnight fox* (Puffin)
COOKSON, Catherine   *Joe and the gladiator* (Puffin)
        The nipper (Puffin)
DAHL, Roald   *Danny the champion of the world* (Puffin)
* EDWARDS, Dorothy   *My naughty little sister* (Magnet)
FARMER, Penelope   *Charlotte sometimes* (Puffin)
* FOX, Mem   *Wilfrid Gordon McDonald Partridge* (Puffin)
FOX, Paula   *The one-eyed cat* (Piper)
GARDAM, Jane   *The Hollow Land* (Puffin)
GARFIELD, Leon   *The apprentices* (Puffin)
GARNER, Alan   *The stone book quartet* (Collins Lions)
* GODDEN, Rumer   *The story of Holly and Ivy* (Puffin)
HOLM, Anna   *I am David* (Magnet)
HOWKER, Janni   *Badger on the barge* (Collins Lions)
      The nature of the best (Collins Lions)
KLEIN, Robin   *Boss of the pool* (Puffin)
LITTLE, Jean   *Lost and found* (Young Puffin)
† McKINLEY, Robin   *The blue sword* (Futura)
      The hero and the crown (Futura)
† MAHY, Margaret   *The haunting* (Magnet)
      Memory (Puffin Plus)
MARK, Jan   *Thunder and lightnings* (Puffin)
* MATTINGLEY, Christobel   *Duck boy* (Young Puffin)
MORPURGO, Michael   *Why the whales came* (Magnet)
PEARCE, Philippa   *A dog so small* (Puffin)
      Tom's midnight garden (Puffin)
PHIPSON, Joan   *The Grannie season* (Magnet)
† SEBESTYEN, Ouida   *Words by heart* (Hamish Hamilton hb)
STOLZ, Mary   *Cat walk* (Collins Lions)
† VOIGT, Cynthia   *The runner* (Collins Teen Tracks) and related titles
WALSH, Jill Paton   *Fireweed* (Puffin)
      A parcel of patterns (Puffin Plus)
† WRIGHTSON, Patricia   *A little fear* (Puffin)

PICTURE BOOKS

* BROWN, Ruth   *Our cat Flossie* (Anderson Press) hb
BURNINGHAM, John   *Granpa* (Picture Puffin)
* HEDDERWICK, Marie   *Katie Morag delivers the mail* (Picture Lions)
* HUGHES, Shirley   *Dogger* (Picture Lions)
KEEPING, Charles   *Sammy Streetsinger* (OUP) and other titles
* ROSE, Gerald   *The tigerskin rug* (Picture Puffin)
* SMITH, Miriam   *Kimi and the watermelon* (Picture Puffin)

Analyse your book character by ticking the boxes (below). Then, using tracing paper, choose a face shape, hair, and features. Add your own details and clip out your portrait. Stick it in the box. Try another character!

FACE SHAPES	EYES	NOSE	MOUTH	EARS/EYEBROWS etc	HAIR

YOUR NAME: _____

AUTHOR: _____

TITLE: _____

SHAPE OF FACE	ROUND	SQUARE	OVAL	HEAVY JAW	BIG EARS	SMALL EARS		
HAIR	STRAIGHT	CURLY	DARK	FAIR	SHORT	LONG		
EYES	BIG	SMALL	CLOSE TOGETHER	FAR APART	HEAVY LIDS	FRIENDLY	HOSTILE	SCARED
NOSE	BIG	SMALL	FLAT	POINTED	TILTED	AQUILINE	BROAD	
MOUTH	BIG	SMALL	SMILING	ANGRY	SAD	BEMUSED	CYNICAL	
EXPRESSION	KIND	FRIENDLY	SLY	CHEEKY	HAPPY	SAD	FUNNY	

EXAMPLES

CHARACTER'S NAME

CHARACTER'S NAME

CHARACTER'S NAME

Identikits

Use this as a starting point. Features can be added to extend the range of possibilities. If the parts are 'blown up' readers can build up portraits on overhead projector transparencies. As ever, discussion enriches the activity.

AIKEN, Joan   *The wolves of Willoughby Chase* (Puffin) **Dido Twite, Miss Slighcarp**
† ASHLEY, Bernard   *Dodgem* (Puffin) **Simon**
BAWDEN, Nina   *Carrie's war* (Puffin) **Carrie**
BYARS, Betsy   *The cartoonist* (Puffin) **Alfie**
    Cracker Jackson (Puffin) **Cracker and Goat**
    The eighteenth emergency (Puffin) **'Mouse'**
CANNING, Victor   *The runaways* (Puffin) and sequels **Smiler**
CLEARY, Beverly   *Dear Mr. Henshaw* (Puffin) **Leigh**
    *Ramona the pest (Puffin) **Ramona**
CONFORD, Ellen   *Felicia the critic* (Puffin) **Felicia**
COOLIDGE, Susan   *What Katy did* (Puffin Classics) **Katy**
DAHL, Roald   *The BFG* (Puffin) **BFG**
DANZIGER, Paula   *Can you sue your parents for malpractice?* (Piper) **Lauren**
FISK, Nicholas   *Grinny* (Puffin) **Great Aunt Emma**
FITZHURGH, Louise   *Harriet the spy* (Collins Lion) **Harriet**
    Nobody's family is going to change (Collins Lion) **Emma, Willie**
† GARDAM, Jane   *Bilgewater* (Sphere) **Marigold**
GARFIELD, Leon   *Smith* (Puffin) **Smith**
GEORGE, Jean   *My side of the mountain* (Puffin) **Sam**
† HAUTZIG, Esther   *The endless steppe* (Puffin Plus) **Esther**
† HINTON, S.E.   *Tex* (Collins Teen Tracks) **Tex**
HOLM, Anne   *I am David* (Magnet) **David**
HOLMAN, Felice   *Slake's limbo* (Collins Lions) **Slake**
HUGHES, Monica   *The keeper of the Isis light* (Magnet) **Olwen**
KEMP, Gene   *The turbulent term of Tyke Tiler* (Puffin) **Tyke**
† KENNEMORE, Tim   *The fortunate few* (Puffin Plus) **Jodie Bell**
KLEIN, Robin   *Games* (Puffin) **Patricia, Kirsty, Genevieve**
    Hating Alison Ashby (Puffin) **Alison**
LOWRY, Lois   *Anastasia Krupnik* (Collins Lions) **Anastasia**
MAGORIAN, Michelle   *Goodnight Mr Tom* (Puffin) **Willie**
MAHY, Margaret   †*The haunting* (Magnet) **Barney**
    *The great piratical rumbustification (Puffin) **the chief robber**
*MURPHY, Jill   *The worst witch* (Puffin) **Mildred**
PATERSON, Katherine   *The great Gilly Hopkins* (Puffin) **Gilly**
PEARCE, Philippa   *Tom's midnight garden* (Puffin) **Tom**
PEYTON, K.M.   *Froggett's revenge* (Puffin) **Danny**
PILLING, Ann   *The year of the worm* (Puffin) **Peter**
SUTCLIFF, Rosemary   *Warrior Scarlet* (Puffin) **Drem**
VOIGT, Cynthia   *Dicey's song* (Collins Lions) **Dicey and the family**
* WILSON, Forrest   *Supergran* (Puffin) **Supergran**

CASTAWAY CHARACTER

YOU ARE ADRIFT AT SEA ON A SMALL RAFT...
FROM ALL THE BOOKS YOU HAVE READ AND LISTED IN
YOUR READING LOG, CHOOSE ONE CHARACTER TO BE
YOUR COMPANION. WHAT SORT OF PERSON WOULD YOU
CHOOSE? THE SUN IS HOT AND YOUR SUPPLIES ARE
MEAGRE....

Who? Character _____

From (title): _____

By: _____

Why? _____

_____

_____

_____

_____

_____

_____

_____

Castaway Characters

Readers can work out the character (or combination of, say, 3) they would most/least like to have as a shipwreck companion on a raft. Answers make a good basis for group discussion in which members have to justify their choices in terms of personality, skills and temperament, based on reference to the character's behaviour in the book they have read.

AIKEN, Joan   *The teeth of the gale and sequels* (Puffin) **Felix**
ALEXANDER, Lloyd   *The book of three* (Collins Lions) **Taran**
* CARTWIGHT, Ann and Reg   *Norah's ark* (Picture Puffin) **Norah**
CHRISTOPHER, John   *Fireball* (Puffin) **Simon/Brad**
* CLEARY, Beverly   *Romona the pest* (Puffin)
COOPER, Susan   *The dark is rising* and sequels (Puffin) **Will**
CRESSWELL, Helen   *The Bagthorpe saga,* any title (Puffin) **any Bagthorpe**
FARMER, Penelope   *Charlotte sometimes* (Puffin) **either girl**
FITZHUGH, Louise   *Harriet the spy* (Collins Lions) **Harriet**
GARFIELD, Leon   *The December rose* (Puffin) **Barnacle**
GEORGE, Jean   *My side of the mountain* (Puffin) **Sam Bribley**
GIRLING, Brough   *Vera Pratt and the false moustaches* (Puffin) **Mrs Pratt**
GRANT, Gwen   *Private, keep out* (Collins Lions) **any**
† GUY, Rosa   *New guys round the block* (Puffin Plus) **Imamu Jones**
* HOBAN, Russell   *How Tom beat Captain Najork and his hired sportsmen/*
            A near thing for Captain Najork (Piper Flippers) **any**
HOOPER, Mary   *Janey's diary* (Magnet) **Janey**
HUGHES, Monica   *Devil on my back* (Magnet) **Toni**
            The keeper of the Isis light (Magnet) **Owen**
HUNTER, Norman   *Professor Branestawm stories* (Puffin)
† JOHNSON, Pete   *Catch you on the flip side* (Collins Teen Tracks) **Brad**
JONES, Terry   *Nicobobinus* (Puffin)
* KAYE, M.M.   *The ordinary princess* (Puffin) **Princess Amy**
KING, Clive   *Stig of the Dump* (Puffin) **Stig**
* LAVELLE, Sheila   *The fiend next door* (Collins Lions)
LESSON, Robert   *The third class genie* (Collins Lions) **Alec or the genie**
LE GUIN, Ursula   *The wizard of Earthsea* (Puffin) **Ged**
LOWRY, Lois   *Anastasia Krupnik* (Collins Lions)
† MARK, Jan   *Feet* (Puffin Plus) **any**
McBRATNEY, Sam   *Zesty* (Magnet)
* McNAUGHTON, Colin   *King Nonn the Wiser* (Pocket Puffin)
* MAHY, Margaret   *The great piratical rumbustification* (Puffin) **any**
* MURPHY, Jill   *The worst witch* (Puffin) **Mildred**
† PEYTON, K. M.   *Pennington's seventeenth summer* and sequels (Magnet Teens)
PILLING, Ann   *Henry's leg* (Puffin) **Henry**
† SCHLEE, Ann   *The vandal* (Magnet) **Paul**
SPEARE, Elizabeth   *The bronze bow* (Puffin) **Daniel**
TOLKEIN, J.R.R.   *The hobbit* (Unwin pb) **any**
† VOIGHT, Cynthia   *The runner* (Collins Teen Tracks) **Bullet Tillerman**
WALSH, Jill Paton   *The butty boy* (Puffin) **'Harry'**
WESTALL, Robert   *The machine gunners* (Puffin) **Chas McGill**

No one is 100% good or 100% bad. Does your hero/heroine have some faults? Does your villain have some redeeming features? Think about what they did in the story and colour in the bar to rank the % of their good and bad qualities

YOUR NAME: _____ AUTHOR: _____ TITLE: _____

GOOD CHARACTER: _____ INITIAL: ____ BAD CHARACTER: _____ INITIAL: ____

Rank each character on the qualities listed below. Add others in the blanks.

CHARACTERISTIC	INITIAL	PERCENTAGE 0 10 20 30 40 50 60 70 80 90 100	EXAMPLE (Page)
KIND			
KIND			
GENEROUS			
GENEROUS			
CARING			
CARING			
FRIENDLY			
FRIENDLY			
HONEST			
HONEST			
THOUGHTFUL			
THOUGHTFUL			
UNSELFISH			
UNSELFISH			
TRUSTWORTHY			
TRUSTWORTHY			
MEAN			
MEAN			
JEALOUS			
JEALOUS			
SCHEMING			
SCHEMING			
ARROGANT			
ARROGANT			
DISHONEST			
DISHONEST			
THOUGHTLESS			
THOUGHTLESS			
SELFISH			
SELFISH			
UNTRUSTWORTHY			
UNTRUSTWORTHY			

INITIAL / PERCENTAGE 10 20 30 40 50 60 70 80 90 100

GOODIES & BADDIES GRAPH

Goodies and Baddies

STORIES

ASHLEY, Bernard †*All my men* (Puffin) **Paul and Billy**
†*High pavement blues* (Puffin) **Devin and Alfie**
†*A kind of wild justice* (Puffin) **Ronnie and Charlie**
†*Terry on the fence* (Puffin) **Terry and Les**
BYARS, Betsy *The two thousand pound goldfish* (Puffin) **Warren and his mother**
CHAMBERS, Adrian *Seal secret* (Hippo) **William and Glynn**
COWLEY, Joy *The silent one* (Methen hb) **Jonasi and Aesake**
DICKINSON, Peter *Annerton Pit* (Puffin) **Martin and Jake**
GARFIELD, Leon *Black Jack* (Puffin) **Tolly and Black Jack**
Guilt and gingerbread (Puffin) **Giorgio and Princess Charlotte**
† HUGHES, Monica *Sandwriter* (Magnet) **Princes Anita and Jodril**
KLEIN, Robin *Boss of the Pool* (Puffin) **Erica and Alison**
Hating Alison Ashby (Puffin) **Erica and Alison**
McCUTCHEON, Elsie *The rat war* (Dent hb) **Morna and Nicholas**
† MAYNE, William *Drift* (Puffin) **Rafe and Tawena**
PEYTON, K.M. *Froggett's Revenge* (Puffin) **Denny and Wayne**
PILLING, Ann *Year of the worm* (Puffin) **Peter and 'Pig' Baxter**
POTTS, Richard *Battleground* (Hodder & Stoughton hb) **Tod and Barry**
RUBENS, Hilary *Calf of the November cloud* (Piper) **Parmet and Konyek**
SEFTON, Catherine *Shadows on the lake* (Hamish Hamilton hb) **Annie and Baxter**
STREATFEILD, Noel *White Boots* (Puffin) **Harriet and Lala**
* SWINDELLS, Robert *A serpent's tooth* (Hamish Hamilton hb) **Lucy and her parents**

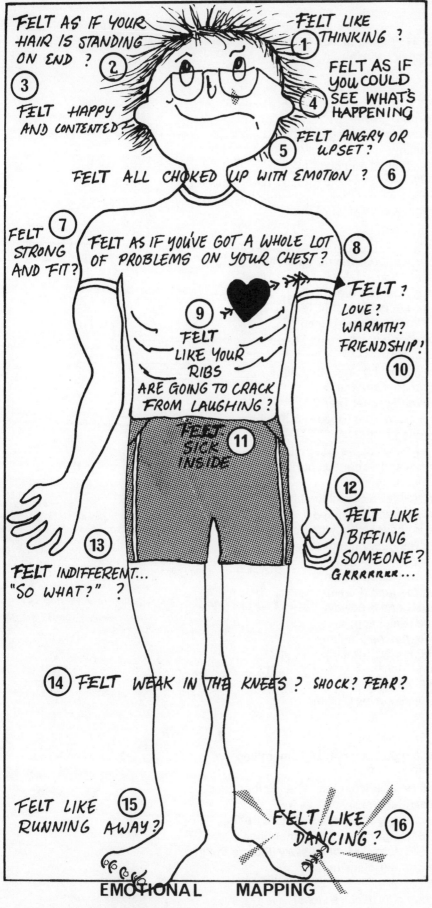

FELT AS IF YOUR HAIR IS STANDING ON END? ②

③ FELT HAPPY AND CONTENTED?

① FELT LIKE THINKING?

④ FELT AS IF YOU COULD SEE WHAT'S HAPPENING

⑤ FELT ANGRY OR UPSET?

FELT ALL CHOKED UP WITH EMOTION? ⑥

⑦ FELT STRONG AND FIT?

FELT AS IF YOU'VE GOT A WHOLE LOT OF PROBLEMS ON YOUR CHEST? ⑧

⑨ FELT LIKE YOUR RIBS ARE GOING TO CRACK FROM LAUGHING?

FELT? LOVE? WARMTH? FRIENDSHIP! ⑩

FELT SICK INSIDE ⑪

⑫ FELT LIKE BIFFING SOMEONE? GRRRRRRR...

⑬ FELT INDIFFERENT... "SO WHAT?"?

⑭ FELT WEAK IN THE KNEES? SHOCK? FEAR?

FELT LIKE RUNNING AWAY? ⑮

FELT LIKE DANCING? ⑯

EMOTIONAL MAPPING

reading is feeling

NAME: _____

When I read _____

by _____

I felt ◯ when _____
_____
_____

I felt ◯ when _____
_____

I felt ◯ when _____
_____

I felt ◯ when _____
_____

I felt ◯ when _____
_____

I felt ◯ when _____
_____
_____

IF YOU FELT ANY OF THE EMOTIONS SHOWN ON THE MAP, FILL IN THE NUMBER IN THE ◯ ABOVE AND SAY WHEN.

Reading is Feeling

A companion activity to Reading as Feeling (p. 23). Older pupils starting on response work may prefer this activity.

STORIES

  ANDERSON, Rachel *The war orphan* (Swallow)
* ASHLEY, Bernard *A bit of give and take* (Young Corgi)
* BERG, Leila *My dog Sunday* (Puffin)
  BYARS, Betsy *After the goatman* (Puffin) and other titles
  CONFORD, Ellen *If this is love I'll take spaghetti* (Collins Teen Tracks)
  DANZIGER, Paula *The cat ate my gymsuit* (Piper) and other titles
  DARKE, Marjorie *The first of Midnight* (Puffin Plus)
† DICKINSON, Peter *Healer* (Puffin Plus)
† DUNCAN, Lois *Stranger with my face* (Pan Horizons) and other titles
* FEAGLES, Anita *Casey the utterly impossible horse* (Puffin)
  HAIGH, Sheila *The little gymnast* (Hippo)
  JONES, Diana Wynn *Dogsbody* (Magnet Teens)
        † *Fire and hemlock* (Magnet Teens)
† KENNEMORE, Tim *Changing Times* (Magnet Teens)
† LILLINGTON, Kenneth *An ash-blonde witch* (Puffin Plus)
† LIVELY, Penelope *Going back* (Puffin)
  McCUTCHEON, Elsie *Storm bird* (Dent hb) and other titles
  MAGORIAN, Michelle *Goodnight Mr Tom* (Puffin)
† MAHY, Margaret *The Changeover* (Magnet Teens)
  MATTINGLEY, Christobel *The miracle tree* (Hodder & Stoughton)
* MORGAN, Alison *Bright-eye* (Young Puffin)
  MORPURGO, Michael *Why the whales came* (Magnet)
  PARK, Ruth *Callie's castle* (Angus and Robertson pb)
* PHIPSON, Joan *The Grannie season* (Magnet)
  POTTS, Richard *Battleground* (Hodder & Stoughton hb)
  RUBENS, Hilary *Calf of the November cloud* (Piper)
  SEFTON, Catherine *Shadows on the lake* (Hamish Hamilton hb)
† SMITH, Rukshana *Rainbows of the gutter* (Magnet Teens)
  SUTCLIFFE, Rosemary *Warrior Scarlet* (Puffin)
        Tristan and Iseult (Puffin)
† SWINDELLS, Robert *Brother in the land* (Puffin)
        Staying up (Corgi Freeway)
  TREECE, Henry *The Dreamtime* (Knight op)
  VAN DER LOEFF, A. *Rutgers Avalanche* (Puffin)
  WALSH, Jill Paton *Gaffer Samson's luck* (Puffin)
        Torch (Puffin)
  WHITE, E. B. *Charlotte's Web* (Puffin)
  WILDER, Laura Ingalls *Little House series* (Puffin)

PICTURE BOOKS

* BROWNE, Anthony *Look what I've got* (Magnet) and other titles
* BURNINGHAM, John *Grandpa* (Picture Puffin)
* COLE, Babette *Princess Smartypants* (Picture Lions) and other titles
  HENRI, Adrian *Eric the punk cat* (Magnet)
* HOWE, James *The day the teacher went bananas* (Picture Puffin)
  KEEPING, Charles *Sammy Streetsinger* (OUP) and other titles
* KORALEK, Jenny and LAWRENCE, John *Mabel's story* (Picture Puffin)
  MORIMOTO, Junko *The white crane* (Collins hb)
  ROSE, Gerald *Scruff* (Magnet)
  VARLEY, Susan *Badger's parting gifts* (Picture Lions)

Banquet of Reading menu

Soup :– a short, smooth read ; goes down easily ; no chewing
(FIND A BOOK FOR EACH COURSE AND GIVE AUTHOR, TITLE, COMMENT OR ★'s)
eg HOBAN, Russell
The twenty – elephant restaurant
★★★★

_____
_____
_____

Entrée :– small, spicy, nutty, lively, crunchy, sizzling ; interesting flavour but you can cope with more :–

_____
_____
_____

Main Course :– full of nourishment for the mind, feelings and imagination ; rich in ideas ; full-bodied characterization ; plot and theme with a subtle flavour ; needs to be chewed slowly !

_____
_____
_____

Dessert :– Light and frothy or rich and creamy or fresh and fruity

_____
_____

Coffee :– Rich mellow flavour to round off a scrumptious meal !

_____
_____

This meal is recommended by : _____

Banquet of Reading

This menu is made up of books which are my personal favourites and which I'd like to share with all children; but tastes differ, so try to provide a wider choice.

Soup – short, smooth read, no chewing; picture books with appeal for all ages

```
* BROWN, Ruth    Our cat Flossie (Anderson Press hb)
  COONEY, Barbara    Miss Rumphius (Julia MacRae hb)
  GOBLE, Paul    The girl who loved wild horses (Picturemac)
* HOBAN, Russell and BLAKE, Quentin    How Tom beat Captain Najork and his hired sportsmen (Cape)
  KLEIN, Robin    Penny Pollard's diary (OUP pb)
```

Entrée – small, spicy, nutty, crunchy, sizzling; whets reading appetite

```
  CROSSLEY-HOLLAND, Keven    Storm (Heinemann Banana Books)
* GAGE, Wilson    Mrs Gaddy and the ghost (Hippo)
  GARFIELD, Leon    The apprentices (Puffin)
  GARNER, Alan    The stone book (Collins Lions)
  HUGHES, Ted    The iron man (Faber pb)
* JOY, Margaret    Hairy and Slug (Young Puffin)
  ROCKWELL, Thomas    How to eat fried worms (Piper)
* UNGERER, Tomi    Moonman (Magnet)
  WAGNER, Jenny and BROOKS, Ron    John Brown, Rose and the midnight cat (Picture Puffin)
* ZION, Gene    Harry the dirty dog (Picture Puffin)
```

Main Course – meaty and nourishment for the mind, feelings and imagination; these need chewing and reading stamina

```
  ANDERSON, Rachel    The poacher's son (Collins Lions)
  BAWDEN, Nina    The peppermint pig (Puffin)
  BURNFORD, Sheila    The incredible journey (Coronet)
  COOPER, Susan    The dark is rising and sequels (Puffin)
  CORBETT, W.J.    The song of Pentecost and sequels (Puffin)
  GEORGE, Jean    Julie and the wolves (Puffin) and other titles
  HOBAN, Russell    The mouse and his child (Puffin)
  HOLM, Anne    I am David (Magnet)
  HOWKER, Janni    Badger on the barge (Collins Lions) and other titles
  KEMP, Gene    The turbulent term of Tyke Tiler (Puffin)
  LE GUIN, Ursula    The wizard of Earthsea (Puffin)
† McKILLIP, Patricia    The riddlemaster of Hed (Orbit) and other titles
† McKINLEY, Robin    The blue sword (Futura) and other titles
† MAHY, Margaret    Memory (Puffin Plus)
  PATERSON, Katherine    A bridge to Terabithia (Puffin)
                        The great Gilly Hopkins (Puffin)
  PEARCE, Philippa    A dog so small (Puffin)
                      Tom's midnight garden (Puffin)
  WALSH, Jill Paton    The dolphin crossing (Puffin) and other titles
```

Dessert and Coffee – round off the meal with a little something to delight and amuse

```
  BROWNE, Anthony    Piggybook (Magnet)
* HOBAN, Russell    Dinner at Alberta's (Puffin)
* LOBEL, Arnold    Ming Lo moves the mountain (Julia MacRae)
* MURPHY, Jill    The worst witch (Puffin)
  RAYNER, Mary    Mr and Mrs Pig's evening out (Macmillan) and other titles
```

bookburgers reading recipes

The best bookburgers are made with only the best ingredients
Choose a book and test the ingredients . . .

chef: _____   **author:** _____

title: _____

ingredients: Rich, beefy, full-flavoured characters ... so clear you feel as if you
know them. Give examples :—

_____

_____

Mixed with : speech, dialogue so clear you feel you can hear them. Quote example :—

_____

_____

_____

Spiced with : description of places so clear you can see them. Quote example :—

_____

_____

_____

Blended into : a subtle plot with an interesting flavour and some surprises. What is it?

_____

_____

_____

Topped with a unique sauce. What makes it different, better for you than others ?

_____

_____

Delicious Nutritious Finger-licking food for the imagination

Served on a bed of crunchy fresh language with a relish of words like :

_____

_____

_____

Exchange recipes with a friend. Become a connoisseur of bookburgers.

Bookburgers

STORIES

AHLBERG, Allan   *Woof* (Puffin)
AIKEN, Joan   *Dido and Pa* and sequels (Cape and Puffin)
       The teeth of the gale and sequels (Puffin)
ALCOCK, Vivien   *Travellers by night* (Collins Lions)
* ARKLE, Phyllis   *The railway cat's secret* (Puffin)
BAILLIE, Alan   *Little brother* (Magnet)
* BROWN, Jeff   *Flat Stanley* (Magnet)
CHRISTOPHER, John   *Fireball* and sequels (Puffin)
       The Tripods triology (Puffin)
COPUS, Martyn   *The ceremony* (Collins Lions)
CROSSLEY-HOLLAND, Kevin   *Storm* (Heinemann Banana Books)
DAVIES, Hunter   *Flossie Teacake strikes back* (Young Lions)
DOHERTY, Berlie   *Children of winter* (Collins Lions)
       White Peak farm (Collins Lions)
FISK, Nicholas   *Antigrav* (Puffin) and other titles
GARFIELD, Leon   *The December Rose* (Puffin)
GEE, Maurice   *The halfmen of O* and sequels (Puffin)
GIRLING, Brough   *Vera Pratt stories* (Puffin)
HARRISON, Harry   *The men from P.I.G. and R.O.B.O.T.* (Puffin)
HOWE, James and Deborah   *Bunnicula* (Young Lions)
HOWKER, Janni   *Badger on the barge* (Collins Lions)
JONES, Terry   *The saga of Erik the Viking* (Puffin)
       Nicobobinus (Puffin)
* JOY, Margaret   *Hairy and Slug* (Puffin)
KING-SMITH, Dick   *Magnus Powermouse* (Puffin) and other titles
KLEIN, Robin   *Ratbags and rascals* (Hippo)
LESSON, Robert   *The third class genie* and sequel (Collins Lions)
LEWIS, C.S.   *The lion, the witch and the wardrobe* (Collins Lions) series
MAHY, Margaret   *Nonstop nonsense* (Magnet)
MARRAY, Denis   *The Duck Street gang* (Magnet)
PEYTON, K.M.   *Who, Sir, Me Sir?* (Puffin)
ROSEN, Michael   *Hairy tales and nursery crimes* (Young Lions)
       Nasty! (Puffin)
SERRAILLIER, Ian   *The silver sword* (Puffin)
       There's no escape (Puffin)
THEROUX, Paul   *A Christmas card* (Puffin)
* WILLIAMS, Ursula Moray   *Jeffy the burglar's cat* (Puffin)
† WRIGHTSON, Patricia   *A little fear* (Puffin)

PICTURE BOOKS

* AARDEMA, Verna   *Bringing the rain to Kapiti Plain* (Picturemac)
CUTLER, Ivor and OXENBURY, Helen   *Meal one* (Piper)
FRENCH, Fiona   *Maid of the Wood* (OUP) and other titles
* KINMONTH, Patrick and CARTWRIGHT, Reg   *Mr Potter's pigeon* (Pocket Puffin)
OAKLEY, Graham   *The Church Mouse* (Picturemac) and series
STEIG, William   *Dr de Soto* (Hippo)

zodiaction

YOUR ZODIAC SIGN:

CAPRICORN
December 21 – January 20

CAUTIOUS • PERSISTENT • DETERMINED • AMBITIOUS • EXPRESSES FEELINGS SENSIBLY • DISLIKES OVER-ENTHUSIASM / PRETENCE • NEEDS ORDER • VALUES STANDARDS • STRIVES TO IMPROVE • HARDWORKING • DUTIFUL • RESPONSIBLE • LIKES SUCCESS / AUTHORITY

AQUARIUS
January 21 – February 19

UNPREDICTABLE • SPONTANEOUS • CARES ABOUT HUMAN BEINGS • LIKES TO BE DIFFERENT • REBELLIOUS • LIKES THE UNUSUAL • EXPRESSES FEELINGS OBJECTIVELY • NEEDS TO EXPERIMENT / TRY THINGS OUT • VALUES IMPARTIALITY • LIKES TO STAND APART

PISCES
February 20 – March 20

SYMPATHETIC • HELPFUL • EXPRESSES FEELINGS SENSITIVELY • SELFLESS • LIKES TO GIVE • SEEKS DEVOTION • IDEALISTIC • LIKES FANTASY • IMAGINATIVE • VALUES LOVE • POETIC • DOES NOT LIKE CRITICISM • ROMANTIC • DREAMY • COMPASSIONATE

ARIES
March 21 – April 20

IMPETUOUS • LIKES CHALLENGE • ENERGETIC • BOLD • LIKES TO WIN • ENTHUSIASTIC • EXPRESSES FEELINGS IMMEDIATELY • SINCERE • DIRECTNESS • NEEDS GOALS • VALUES • DOESN'T LIKE UNIFORMITY / ORDER • SELF-SUFFICIENT • INDEPENDENT

SAGGITARIUS
November 23 – December 21

HONEST • EXPRESSES FEELINGS OPENLY / WARMLY • WARMTH • VALUES INDEPENDENCE • VALUES FREEDOM • THREATENED BY TIES IN A LOT • LIKES TO UNDERSTAND • SEEKS KNOWLEDGE • LIKES ADVENTURE • PHILOSOPHIC • TOLERANT • OUTGOING

TAURUS
April 21 – May 21

CAUTIOUS • STEADY • DOESN'T TAKE RISKS • CALM • SLOW TO EXPRESS FEELINGS • LIKES TO OWN LOTS OF THINGS • LIKES TO KNOW A LOT • NEEDS CALM AND SECURITY • STABILITY • LIKES ROUTINE • EMOTIONAL • DOESN'T LIKE CHANGE • UNPREDICTABLE • MOODY • CHANGEABLE

SCORPIO
October 24 – November 22

INTENSE • POWERFUL • PASSIONATE • NEEDS TO EXPRESS FEELINGS • LIKES TO DEFEAT • DEEP • PROFOUND • THINKS DEEPLY • DOESN'T LIKE THOUGHTS AND FEELINGS TO BE DISCOVERED BY OTHERS • SEEKS POWER • LIKES CHALLENGE • MAGNETIC • DYNAMIC • PRIVATE

GEMINI
May 22 – June 22

VERSATILE • IN LOTS OF THINGS • LIKES TO COMMUNICATE • ENJOYS NEW SERVICES • CHANGE • NEEDS NOVELTY • INTERESTED • EXCITABLE • FLEXIBLE • LIKES CHANGE • CHANGE • SHY • FINDS IT DIFFICULT TO COMMUNICATE • CARING • IF PEOPLE WITHDRAW • FEELS THREATENED • LIKE FAMILIAR

LIBRA
September 24 – October 23

EASY-GOING • LUCKY • LIKES CO-OPERATIVE • LIKES TO RELATE TO PEOPLE • DIPLOMATIC • HAPPY • PLEASANT / PEACEFUL • COMPANY • TRAIT • LIKES FAIRNESS • EXPRESSES PLEASANTLY • JUSTICE • LIKES TO BE PERFECT • INDECISION • DISCRIMINATION • NEEDS UNITY • VALUES PEACE

CANCER
June 22 – July 23

SENSITIVE • RELIABLE • NEEDS TO BE LOVED AND CHERISHED • DEVOTED • DOESN'T LIKE CHANGE / LIKES TO PROTECT • CARES DEEPLY • NOT SHY • COMMUNICATES EASILY • NEEDS TO BE APPRECIATED • THREATENED BY INDIFFERENCE • OPEN • PROUD

VIRGO
August 24 – September 23

CONSCIENTIOUS • LIKES PERFECTION • RESPONSIBLE • PAINSTAKING • HATES UNTIDINESS • EXPRESSES DELICATE FEELINGS • SELECTIVELY • CAUTIOUSLY • LIKES THINGS WANTS TO PERFECT • EFFICIENCY • LIKES ORDER • DUTIFUL • SEEKS ORDER • CRITICAL • LIKES RESEARCH

LEO
July 24 – August 23

IMPULSIVE • GENEROUS • WARM • SPONTANEOUS • LIKES ADMIRATION • DRAMATIC • LIKES BIG IDEAS • LIKES TO BE A LEADER

LEO

SUPERSTITIOUS NONSENSE & UTTER HOCUS POCUS

• CHOOSE A BOOK • CHOOSE A CHARACTER • BORN UNDER WHICH SIGN OF THE ZODIAC?

AUTHOR:

TITLE:

NAME OF CHARACTER:

HER/HIS SIGN OF THE ZODIAC IS:

I think _____ was born under _____ because

Zodiaction

As this activity relies on experience of astrology and horoscopes it is probably best restricted to readers over 10. The data is not authentic and is not intended to be taken seriously. It is intended to act as a catalyst for discussion of interesting book characters.

Characters listed in GOODIES AND BADDIES, IDENTIKITS, A LETTER TO A BOOK CHARACTER, CASTAWAY CHARACTER and PRUNELLA PROBLEM would also be suitable for this activity. If several readers are working on the same title it is interesting for them to compare their analyses and justify them in terms of what happens in the book, how their character reacts, and so on.

ANDERSON, Rachel   *The poacher's son* (Collins Lions) **Arthur Betts**
ASHLEY, Bernard   *A bit of give and take* (Young Corgi) **Scott**
                      The trouble with Donovan Croft (Puffin) **both boys**
BYARS, Betsy   *The eighteenth emergency* (Puffin) **'Mouse'**
* CLEARY, Beverly   *Ramona the pest* (Puffin)
CONFORD, Ellen   *Felicia the critic* (Puffin)
COOPER, Susan   *The dark is rising* (Puffin) **Will**
COPUS, Martyn   *The ceremony* (Collins Lions) **Terry Williams**
† CROSS, Gillian   *Chartbreak* (Puffin Plus) **Janis Finch**
DAHL, Roald   *Danny and the champion of the world* (Puffin) **Danny/his father**
† DARKE, Marjorie   *Comeback* (Puffin Plus) **Gail**
DUDER, Tessa   *Jellybean* (Puffin) **Geraldine**
FITZHUGH, Louise   *Harriet the spy* (Collins Lions)
                      Nobody's family is going to change (Collins Lions) **Emma/Willie**
GEORGE, Jean   *Julie of the wolves* (Puffin) **Julie/Miyax**
HOLMAN, Felice   *Slake's limbo* (Collins Lions) **Slake**
† HOWKER, Janni   *The nature of the beast* (Collins Lions) **Bill**
† HUNTER, Mollie   *I'll go my own way* (Collins Teen Tracks) **Cat McPhie**
KEMP, Gene   *Charlie Lewis plays for time* (Puffin)
                      The turbulent term of Tyke Tiler (Puffin) **Tyke**
† KENNEMORE, Time   *The fortunate few* (Puffin Plus) **Jodie Bell**
LINGARD, Joan   *The twelfth day of July* (Puffin) **Sadie/Nick/Kevin**
McBRATNEY, Sam   *Zesty* (Magnet)
MAHY, Margaret   *Memory* (Puffin Plus) **Johnny**
MARK, Jan   *Thunder and Lightnings* (Puffin) **Andrew, Victor**
† MAYNE, William   *Drift* (Puffin) **Tawena/Rafe**
                      Winter Quarters (Puffin) **Lal/Issy**
PEARCE, Philipa   *The way to Sattin shore* (Puffin) **Kate**
PILLING, Ann   *Henry's leg* (Puffin)
                      The year of the worm (Puffin) **Peter**
† SCHLEE, Ann   *The vandal* (Magnet) **Paul**
* THOMPSON, Kay   *Eloise* (Young Puffin)
TOWNSEND, Sue   *The secret diary of Adrian Mole . . .* (Methuen)
† VOIGT, Cynthia   *Homecoming* (Collins Lions) **Dicey and siblings**
WALSH, Jill Paton   *The butty boy* (Puffin) **'Harry'**

Prunella Problem
COLUMNIST,
COUNSELLOR,
FRIEND

NAME: _____

Imagine that you are a character in the book you have just read. Write a letter to Prunella's column describing your situation and asking for advice. Write Prunella's reply yourself, or give it to a friend to reply if she/he has also read the book.

TITLE: _____

PRUNELLA PROBLEM AUTHOR: _____

Dear Miss Problem of Prunella's Problem Page,
    My name is _____ and I am writing to you because I've got this big problem.

_____

_____

_____

_____

_____

_____

_____

_____

Signed _____

Reply | Dear _____

_____

_____

_____

_____

_____

_____

_____

_____

With my best wishes, Prunella Problem

Prunella Problem

One student can write both the letter and the reply; or two students can read the same book, with one writing the letter, the other the reply.

ALCOCK, Vivienne   *The cuckoo sister* (Collins Lions)
ALCOTT, Louisa May   *Little Women* (Puffin Classics)
ANDERSON, Rachel   *The war orphan* (Swallow)
AVERY, Gillian   *The warden's niece* (Bodley Bookshelf)
BLUME, Judy   *Are you there, God, it's me Margaret* (Piper)
          *Superfudge (Piper)
          Then again maybe I won't (Piper)
          †*Tiger Eyes* (Piper)
BYARS, Betsy   *Cracker Jackson* (Puffin)
          The eighteenth emergency (Puffin) and other titles
CLEARY, Beverly   *Dear Mr. Henshaw* (Puffin)
CONFORD, Ellen   *Felicia the critic* (Puffin)
          If this is love I'll take spaghetti (Collins Teen Tracks)
DANZIGER, Paula   *Can you sue your parents for malpractice?* (Piper)
          The cat ate my gymsuit (Piper)
          The divorce express (Piper)
DUDER, Tessa   *Jellybean* (Puffin)
FINE, Anne   *The Granny project* (Magnet)
FITZHUGH, Louise   *Nobody's family is going to change* (Collins Lions)
HAIGH, Sheila   *The little gymnast* (Hippo)
HALL, Willis   *The return of the antelope* (Young Lions)
* HENDRY, Diana   *Fiona finds her tongue* (Young Puffin)
HILL, Lorna   *A dream of Sadlers Wells* (Piper)
† HINTON, Nigel   *Collision course* (Puffin)
* HOLIDAY, Jane   *Victor the Vulture* (Young Puffin)
† HUGHES, Monica   *The keeper of the Isis light* (Magnet)
KENNEMORE, Till   *Wall of words* (Puffin)
KLEIN, Robin   *Hating Alison Ashby* (Puffin) and other titles
LAVELLE, Sheila   *My best fiend* (Young Lions) and sequel
† LITTLE, Jean   *Mama's going to buy you a mocking bird* (Puffin)
MARK, Jan   *Dead Letter Box (Young Puffin)
          Handles (Puffin)
* MAYNE, William   *No more school* (Puffin)
NEEDLE, Jan   *Losers Weepers* (Magnet)
PATERSON, Katherine   *The great Gilly Hopkins* (Puffin)
PARK, Ruth   *Playing Beatie Bow* (Puffin)
* PEYTON, K.M.   *Going Home* (Magnet)
POWLING, Chris Mog and the Rectifier (Knight)
RODGERS, Mary   *Freaky Friday; Summer Switch* (both Puffin)
SEFTON, Catherine   *The Emma dilemma* (Magnet)
* SINCLAIR, Olga   *Gypsy girl* (Young Lions)
STREATFEILD, Noel   *Ballet Shoes* (Puffin)
TAYLOR, WILLIAM   *My summer of the lions* (Puffin Plus)
† VOIGT, Cynthia   *Homecoming and sequels* (Collins Lions)
† WERSBA, Barbara   *Crazy Vanilla* (Pan Horizons)
* YEOMAN, John and BLAKE, Quentin   *The boy who sprouted antlers* (Young Lions)

DATABASE DATING

Your name: ....

AUTHOR ....

TITLE ....

BOOK CHARACTER'S NAME ....

CHARACTER ANALYSIS

PHYSICAL

Female	
Male	
Short	
Tall	
Dark	
Fair	
Slim	
Sturdy	
Thin	
Weedy	
Pretty	
Handsome	
Lithe	
Slow moving	
Plain	
Ordinary looking	
Special looking	
Stunning	
All round average	

Other

OVERALL CHARACTER TYPE

Extrovert, gregarious	
Introvert, loner	
Warm, bubbly, friendly	
Shy, withdrawn, silent	
Steady, hardworking, reliable	
Impulsive, flipperty, fun	
Emotional, shows feelings	
Reserved, deep feelings	
Arty, imaginative	
Hearty, sporty	
Indoor type	
Outdoor type	

PERSONALITY

Pleasant	
Friendly	
Kind	
Helpful	
Loving	
Fair	
Gentle	
Full of laughter	
Responsible	
Sincere	
Steady	
Placid	
Happy	
Well balanced	
Generous	
Thoughtful	
Unpleasant	
Unfriendly	
Unkind	
Obnoxious	
Rude	
Unlovable	
Tough	
Mean	
Unfair	
Insincere	
Serious, no humour	
Impetuous	
Unhappy	
Jealous	
Silly	
Thoughtless	
Selfish	
Irresponsible	
Spiteful	
Conscientious	
Scatterbrain	

AGE ....

NATIONALITY ....

Database Dating

This can be used in several ways. One reader can read her/his character analysis point by point to the class, with the rest of the students counting each time a tick coincides until the most similar partner is chosen. Classes with access to a computer can design fields, enter data from one book character each and interrogate the database. Alternatives are to find an opposite pair or, using the second list, the most ridiculous match. You could extend this into a written activity by asking students to write an account of the date, using the behaviour of the character in the original book as their information source.

GIRLS

1 FITZHUGH, Louise *Harriet the spy* (Collins Lions) **Harriet**
2 GEORGE, Jean *Julie of the wolves* (Puffin) **Julie/Miyax**
3 HOOPER, Mary *Janey's Diary* (Magnet) **Janey**
4† KENNEMORE, Tim *The fortunate few* (Puffin Plus) **Jodie**
5† KERR, M.E. *Dinky Hocker shoots smack* (Puffin Plus) **Dinky**
6 LINGARD, Joan *The clearance* (Beaver) **Maggie**
7 MARK, Jan *Handles* (Puffin) **Erica**
8 O'DELL, Scott *Island of the blue Dolphins* (Puffin) **Karana**
9 PATERSON, Katherine *The great Gilly Hopkins* (Puffin) **Gilly**
10† STEWART, Maureen *Orange Wendy* (Puffin Plus) **Wendy**

BOYS

1 CANNING, Victor *The runaway and sequels* (Puffin) **Smiler**
2 GEORGE, Jean *My side of the mountain* (Puffin) **Sam**
3† HINTON, S.E. *Tex* (Collins Teen Tracks) **Tex**
4† WESTALL, Robert *Futuretrack 5* (Puffin) **Henry**
5 PILLING, ANN *Henry's leg* (Puffin) **Henry**
6 STEWART, Maureen *Love from Greg* (Puffin Plus) **Greg**
7 TOWNSEND, Sue *The secret diary of Adrian Mole* (Methuen) **Adrian**
8 TULLY, John *Johnny Goodlooks* (Methuen hb) **Johnny**
9† URE, Jean *A proper little Nooryef* (Puffin Plus) **Jamie**
10† VOIGT, Cynthia *The runner* (Collins Lions) **Bullet**

Ridiculous Romances

FEMALE

1 *AHLBERG, Allan *Miss Dose the doctor's daughter* (Puffin)
2 *Mrs Plus the plumber* (Puffin)
3 *CLEARY, Beverly *Ramona the pest* (Puffin)
4 *EDWARDS, Dorothy *My naughty little sister* (Magnet)
5 LINDGREN, Astrid *Pippi Longstocking* (Puffin)
6 PROYSEN, Alf *Mrs Pepperpot* (Puffin)
7 SLEIGH, Barbara *Carbonel* (Puffin)
8 *THOMPSON, Kay *Eloise* (Puffin)
9 TRAVERS, P.L. *Mary Poppins* (Puffin)
10 WILSON, Forrest *SuperGran* (Puffin)

MALE

1 *AHLBERG, Allan *Burglar Bill* (Picture Lions)
2 *BROWN, Jeff *Flat Stanley* (Magnet)
3 DAHL, Roald *The BFG* (Puffin)
4 HUGHES, Ted *The iron man* (Faber)
5 HUNTER, Norman *Professor Branestawm* (Puffin)
6 JANSSON, Tove *The exploits of Moominpappa* (Puffin)
7 LIVELY, Penelope *The ghost of Thomas Kempe* (Puffin)
8 LOFTING, Hugh *Dr Dolittle* (Puffin)
9 TODD, Barbara Euphan *Worzel Gummidge* (Puffin)
10 WILSON, Bob *Stanley Bagshaw books* (Puffin)

This activity also adapts well for older (12–14) reluctant readers of both sexes using picture book pairings. For instance Aunt Fidget Wonkham Strong and Miss Bundlejoy Cosysweet (from Hoban's *How Tom beat Captain Najork and his hired sportsmen*) or Red Riding Hood (from Dahl's *Revolting Rhymes*) could be paired with Arthur (from Hoban's *Dinner at Alberta's*) or Little Tim (from the Edward Ardizzone stories) or Raymond Briggs' Father Christmas. Making animal pairings can also be amusing, for example Toad (from *Wind in the willows*) and Mrs Frisby (from *Mrs Frisby and the rats of NIMH*) or Angelina Ballerina (Katherine Holabird's mouse) and Beatrix Potter's Peter Rabbit or Tom Kitten.

THIS IS YOUR LIFE!

Dear ....,

We are putting together a THIS IS YOUR LIFE programme on ....

Please could you assist us by completing the following biographical details:

<u>Born</u> (approximate or exact date) .... <u>Siblings</u> ....

<u>Where</u> (town, country) ....

<u>Parents</u> .... <u>Brought up by</u> ....

<u>Education</u> ....

<u>Achievements</u> ....

....

....

....

....

....

....

....

....

....

....

We would appreciate it if you would list the people whom you think should be invited to appear on the programme and say how and why he or she was important in the life of this person:

NAME ....

Why ....

....

NAME ....

Why ....

....

NAME ....

Why ....

....

This is Your Life

This activity can be done using biographies, autobiographies, fictionalised fact, biographical and autobiographical stories. It can be combined with further research and with comparison of information from more than one source. The result lends itself to oral presentation, perhaps as a television programme.

PEOPLE

ANNIE BESANT, Olivia Bennet 'In her own time' series (Hamish Hamilton) hb
IAN BOTHAM, Andrew Langley 'Profiles' series (Hamish Hamilton) hb
EDITH CAVELL, Nigel Richardson 'Profiles' (Hamish Hamilton) hb
MARIE CURIE, Angela Bull 'Profiles' (Hamish Hamilton) hb
ROALD DAHL, Chris Powling (Puffin)
        Boy (Puffin) autobiography
        Going solo (Puffin) autobiography
GRACE DARLING, Helen Cresswell (Puffin)
ANN FRANK, Angela Bull 'Profiles' (Hamish Hamilton) hb
        Richard Tames 'Lifelines' (Watts)
        The Diary of Ann Frank (Piccolo)
HELEN KELLER, Carolyn Sloan 'Profiles,' (Hamish Hamilton) hb
        Richard Tames 'Lifelines' (Watts)
MARY SEACOLE, Maudlyn Lewis 'In her own time' series (Hamish Hamilton) hb
MOTHER TERESA, Richard Tames 'Lifelines' (Watts)
ROBIN HOOD, Edward Blishen (Knight)
        Antonia Fraser (Magnet)
        Catherine Storr (Methuen Long Ago series)
        Roger Lancelyn Green (Puffin Classics)
        Julian Atterton (Julia MacRae Redwing series)

FICTIONALISED FACT/BIOGRAPHICAL STORIES

ALCOTT, Louisa *Little Women,* (Puffin Classics) and sequels
† DARKE, Marjorie *The first of Midnight* (Puffin Plus) and sequels
† DOROTHY, Berlie *Granny was a buffer girl* (Collins Teen Tracks)
GARDAM, Jane *The Hollow Land* (Puffin)
† HAUTZIG, Esther *The endless steppe* (Puffin Plus)
HOROWITZ, Anthony *The new adventures of William Tell* (Puffin)
HUDSON, JAN *Sweetgrass* (Spindlewood) hb
† KENNEMORE, Tim *The Fortunate Few* (Puffin Plus)
† KOEHN, Ilse Mischling *Second degree* (Puffin Plus)
LESTER, Julius *Long journey home* (Puffin)
        To be a slave (Puffin)
MACLACHLAN, Patricia *Sarah plain and tall* (Puffin)
MARSHALL, Alan *I can jump puddles* (Puffin Plus)
O'DELL, Scott *Streams to the river, river to the sea* (Puffin)
PEYTON, K. M. *Flambards series* (Puffin)
† RICHTER, Hans Peter *Friedrich* (Puffin)
SUTCLIFFE, Rosemary *Dragon Slayer: Beowulf* (Puffin)
        The high deeds of Finn McCool (Puffin)
        Song for a dark queen (Boedicea) (Knight)
† TAYLOR, Mildred *Let the circle be unbroken* (Puffin Plus)
        Roll of thunder hear my cry (Puffin Plus)
THOMPSON, B. *Trooper Jackson* (Puffin)
WILDER, Laura Ingalls *Farmer Boy* (Puffin)
        The first four years (Puffin)
        These happy golden years (Puffin)

COUNTRY COUPLES

Read the books suitable for your age group and try to pair the two set in the same country:

TITLE	TITLE	COUNTRY
Example: GEE, Maurice, *Under the mountain* (Puffin)	De Hamel, Joan *X marks the spot* (Puffin)	New Zealand
Book 1	Book 2	
Book 1	Book 2	
Book 1	Book 2	
Book 1	Book 2	
Book 1	Book 2	
Book 1	Book 2	

Country Couples

* AFRICA
LEWIN, Hugh & KOPPER, Lisa   *An elephant came to swim* (Hamish Hamilton) hb **Zimbab**
AARDEMA, Verna   *Bringing the rain to Kapiti Plain* (Picturemac) **Kenya**
RUBENS, Hilary   *Calf of the November cloud* (Piper) **Kenya**
KAYE, Geraldine   *Comfort herself* (Magnet)**Ghana**
DALY, Nicki   *Not so fast Songololo* (Picture Puffin) **South Africa**
NAIDOO, Beverley   *Journey to Jo'burg* (Lions) **South Africa**
HARRIES, Ann   *The sound of the Gora* (Heinemann) **South Africa**
JONES, Toecky   *Go well, stay well* (Puffin) **South Africa**

* AMERICAN INDIAN:
GOBLE, Paul   *The girl who loved wild horses* (Picturemac)
LeCAIN, Errol & LONGFELLOW, Henry Wadsworth
Hiawatha's Childhood (Picture Puffin)
HUDSON, Jan   *Sweetgrass* (Spindlewood)
GOBLE, Paul   any titles (Picturemac)

USA (PIONEER)
WADDELL, Martin   *Going West* (Picture Puffin)
WILDER, Laura Ingalls   *Little House series* (Puffin)

USA (SLAVERY)
LESTER, Julius   *To be a slave* (Puffin)
SMUCKE, Barbara   *Underground to Canada* (Puffin)

USA
GREENE, Betty   *Get on out of here, Philip Hall* (Puffin)
GUY, Rosa   *Paris, Pee Wee and Big Dog* (Puffin)
SEBESTYEN, Ouida   *Words by heart* (Hamish Hamilton) hb
GUY, Rosa   *The friends* (Puffin)

* AUSTRALIA
WAKEFIELD, S.A.   *Bottersnikes and Gumbles* (Piper)
WAGNER, Jenny   *The Bunyip of Berkeley's Creek* (Picture Puffin)

* CARIBBEAN
AGARD, John   *Dig away, Two-hole Tim* (Bodley Head) **Guyana**
BERRY, James   *A thief in the village* (Puffin) **Jamaica**

* CHINA
LOBEL, Arnold   *Ming Lo moves the mountain* (Julia MacRae)
SVEND, Otto S.   *Children of the Yangtze river* (Pelham)

INUIT
GEORGE, Jean   *Julie of the wolves* (Puffin)
MAYNE, William   *Drift* (Puffin)

* INDIA
BOND, Ruskin   *Flames in the forest, Getting Granny's glasses* (Puffin)
BONNICI, Peter   *The first rains* (Bell and Hyman)
DESAI, Anita   *The village by the sea* (Puffin Plus)
JAFFREY, Madhur   *Seasons of splendour* (Pavilion)

* NEW ZEALAND
GRACE, Patricia   *The Kuia and the spider* (Picture Puffin)
SMITH, Miriam   *Kiwi and the watermelon* (Picture Puffin)
De HAMEL, Joan   *Take the long path* (Puffin)
TAYLOR, William   *Summer of the Lions* (Puffin Plus)

* ENGLAND (VICTORIAN)
GARFIELD, Leon   *The December Rose* (Puffin)
LIVELY, Penelope   *Fanny and the monsters* (Puffin)

† EUROPE (WW2)
REISS, Johanna   *The upstairs room* (Puffin)
Richter, Hans Peter   *Freidrich* (Puffin)

In all cases the picture which these books offer of each setting is worth discussing and evaluating. Information from other sources – television, newspapers, magazines etc. can be referred to; the idea of different kinds of writing, of the fact/fiction relationship can be explored.

STUDENT VIEW OF READING : QUESTIONNAIRE

NAME _____ CLASS _____

CROSS OUT WHAT DOES NOT APPLY

I think reading is important / I do not think reading is important
because _____
_____
_____
_____

I enjoy reading / I do not enjoy reading because _____
_____

I read a lot / I read very little because _____
_____

I prefer reading fiction / I prefer reading non-fiction / I like reading both because
_____

Why read? What purpose does reading serve?
To _____
To _____
To _____
To _____

Do you like stories which :

Make you laugh ?	Yes / No
Make you cry ?	Yes / No
Make you think hard ?	Yes / No
Make you feel like the book character ?	Yes / No
Are about people like you and their problems ?	Yes / No
Are about everyday life ?	Yes / No
Are about friends ?	Yes / No
Are set in other countries ?	Yes / No
Are set in the past ?	Yes / No
Are about animals, not people ?	Yes / No
Are about real people ?	Yes / No
Are about space, aliens, the future ?	Yes / No

How do you feel about yourself as a reader ? [Tick box]

GREAT WHOOPEE REALLY OK ☐

SO SO SORT OF OK MIDDLING ☐

BLEH! YUK! DEPRESSED DOWN ☐

Further Reading

BENTON, Michael and FOX, Geoff   *Teaching Literature 9–14* OUP 1985
A very user-friendly guide for any teacher thinking about developing classroom practice. Practical examples and things to do firmly rooted in sound principles which are made accessible and exciting. Good on response.

CHAMBERS, Aidan   *Booktalk* Bodley Head 1985.
One of the most useful books for stimulating 'why read?' discussion.

CLARK, Margaret   *Young fluent readers* Heinemann 1976.
Evidence that children learn to read by reading and being read to, documented in readable research.

FRY, Donald   *Children talk about books: seeing themselves as readers* Open University Press, 1985.
In-depth conversations with six young readers, aged 8, 12 and 15, about their reading. Shows a powerful connection between reading and life!

MEEK, Margaret   *Learning to read* Bodley Head 1986
The reading process explained and children's reading development described, analysed and illustrated. Written for parents; very useful for teachers.

MEEK, Margaret   *How texts teach what readers learn* Thimble Press 1988
A convincing proof of the necessary connection between literature and literacy. Shows by example the reading lessons to be found in books.

MEEK, Margaret (ED.)   *The cool web* London: Bodley Head 1978.
A collection of writings on children's reading and books. No ready remedies, but complex and challenging issues examined with insight and sympathy.

MOSS, Elain   *Part of the pattern* London: Bodley Head 1986.
A lucid and fascinating guide to children's books of the 60s to 80s.

PROTHEROUGH, Robert   *Developing response to fiction* Milton Keynes: Open University Press 1986.
Interesting look at individual readers and their reading responses.

Review Sources

Books for keeps 1 Effingham Road, Lee, London SE12 8NZ
In 6 annual issues there are short helpful reviews with an emphasis on paperbacks, excellent authorgraphs and short articles targeted to teachers.

The Signal selection of children's books Thimble Press, Lockwood Station Rd, South Woodchester, Stroud, Gloucester GL5 5EZ. (Annual).
Annual listing of new books selected by panel of teachers, librarians, etc.

Other Sources

Other review journals and periodicals include *Children's literature in education* (UK/USA), *Signal, School Librarian, Growing Point, Junior Bookshelf.*

READERSHIP AWARD

Awarded to: _____

For excellent response to ~

_____

by _____

Signed _____

Date _____

Have you seen the companion volume to *Reading Alive?*

Library Alive!
Promoting reading and research in the school library

An invaluable resource book for the teacher and librarian, Library Alive! is packed with challenging and absorbing activities to help children learn the skills they need to become confident, independent readers and borrowers – above all to enjoy using books.

It includes games and activities to encourage critical and evaluative skills, research using many kinds of books and resources, and a knowledge of the organisation of a library. The 'planner' and 'skills index' make this book particularly helpful for non-specialists.

The book contains resource and activity material which may be photocopied and distributed for classroom use.